MANHATTAN GMAT

Fractions, Decimals, & Percents

GMAT Strategy Guide

This guide provides an in-depth look at the variety of GMAT questions that test your knowledge of fractions, decimals, and percents. Learn to see the connections among these part–whole relationships and practice implementing strategic shortcuts.

guide **1**

Fractions, Decimals, & Percents GMAT Strategy Guide, Fifth Edition

10-digit International Standard Book Number: 1-935707-63-9
13-digit International Standard Book Number: 978-1-935707-63-9
eISBN: 978-1-937707-04-0

Layout Design: Dan McNaney and Cathy Huang
Cover Design: Evyn Williams and Dan McNaney
Cover Photography: Alli Ugosoli

INSTRUCTIONAL GUIDE SERIES

0   **GMAT Roadmap**
(ISBN: 978-1-935707-69-1)

1   **Fractions, Decimals, & Percents**
(ISBN: 978-1-935707-63-9)

2   **Algebra**
(ISBN: 978-1-935707-62-2)

3   **Word Problems**
(ISBN: 978-1-935707-68-4)

4   **Geometry**
(ISBN: 978-1-935707-64-6)

5   **Number Properties**
(ISBN: 978-1-935707-65-3)

6   **Critical Reasoning**
(ISBN: 978-1-935707-61-5)

7   **Reading Comprehension**
(ISBN: 978-1-935707-66-0)

8   **Sentence Correction**
(ISBN: 978-1-935707-67-7)

9   **Integrated Reasoning & Essay**
(ISBN: 978-1-935707-83-7)

SUPPLEMENTAL GUIDE SERIES

Math GMAT Supplement Guides

Foundations of GMAT Math
(ISBN: 978-1-935707-59-2)

Advanced GMAT Quant
(ISBN: 978-1-935707-15-8)

Official Guide Companion
(ISBN: 978-0-984178-01-8)

Verbal GMAT Supplement Guides

Foundations of GMAT Verbal
(ISBN: 978-1-935707-01-9)

MANHATTAN
GMAT

April 24th, 2012

Dear Student,

Thank you for picking up a copy of *Fractions, Decimals, & Percents*. I hope this book provides just the guidance you need to get the most out of your GMAT studies.

As with most accomplishments, there were many people involved in the creation of the book you are holding. First and foremost is Zeke Vanderhoek, the founder of Manhattan GMAT. Zeke was a lone tutor in New York when he started the company in 2000. Now, 12 years later, the company has instructors and offices nationwide and contributes to the studies and successes of thousands of students each year.

Our Manhattan GMAT Strategy Guides are based on the continuing experiences of our instructors and students. For this volume, we are particularly indebted to Dave Mahler and Stacey Koprince. Dave Mahler deserves special recognition for his contributions over the past number of years. Dan McNaney and Cathy Huang provided their design expertise to make the books as user-friendly as possible, and Noah Teitelbaum and Liz Krisher made sure all the moving pieces came together at just the right time. And there's Chris Ryan. Beyond providing additions and edits for this book, Chris continues to be the driving force behind all of our curriculum efforts. His leadership is invaluable. Finally, thank you to all of the Manhattan GMAT students who have provided input and feedback over the years. This book wouldn't be half of what it is without your voice.

At Manhattan GMAT, we continually aspire to provide the best instructors and resources possible. We hope that you will find our commitment manifest in this book. If you have any questions or comments, please email me at dgonzalez@manhattanprep.com. I'll look forward to reading your comments, and I'll be sure to pass them along to our curriculum team.

Thanks again, and best of luck preparing for the GMAT!

Sincerely,

Dan Gonzalez
President
Manhattan GMAT

HOW TO ACCESS YOUR ONLINE RESOURCES

If you...

▶ **are a registered Manhattan GMAT student**

and have received this book as part of your course materials, you have AUTOMATIC access to ALL of our online resources. This includes all practice exams, question banks, and online updates to this book. To access these resources, follow the instructions in the Welcome Guide provided to you at the start of your program. Do NOT follow the instructions below.

▶ **purchased this book from the Manhattan GMAT online store or at one of our centers**

1. Go to: www.manhattanprep.com/gmat/studentcenter.

2. Log in using the username and password used when your account was set up.

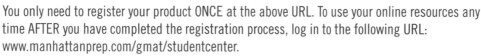

▶ **purchased this book at a retail location**

1. Create an account with Manhattan GMAT at the website: www.manhattanprep.com/gmat/register.

2. Go to: www.manhattanprep.com/gmat/access.

3. Follow the instructions on the screen.

Your one year of online access begins on the day that you register your book at the above URL.

You only need to register your product ONCE at the above URL. To use your online resources any time AFTER you have completed the registration process, log in to the following URL: www.manhattanprep.com/gmat/studentcenter.

Please note that online access is nontransferable. This means that only NEW and UNREGISTERED copies of the book will grant you online access. Previously used books will NOT provide any online resources.

▶ **purchased an eBook version of this book**

1. Create an account with Manhattan GMAT at the website: www.manhattanprep.com/gmat/register.

2. Email a copy of your purchase receipt to gmat@manhattanprep.com to activate your resources. Please be sure to use the same email address to create an account that you used to purchase the eBook.

For any technical issues, email techsupport@manhattanprep.com or call 800-576-4628.

Please refer to the following page for a description of the online resources that come with this book.

YOUR ONLINE RESOURCES

Your purchase includes ONLINE ACCESS to the following:

⊛ 6 Computer-Adaptive Online Practice Exams

The 6 full-length computer-adaptive practice exams included with the purchase of this book are delivered online using Manhattan GMAT's proprietary computer-adaptive test engine. The exams adapt to your ability level by drawing from a bank of more than 1,200 unique questions of varying difficulty levels written by Manhattan GMAT's expert instructors, all of whom have scored in the 99th percentile on the Official GMAT. At the end of each exam you will receive a score, an analysis of your results, and the opportunity to review detailed explanations for each question. You may choose to take the exams timed or untimed.

The content presented in this book is updated periodically to ensure that it reflects the GMAT's most current trends and is as accurate as possible. You may view any known errors or minor changes upon registering for online access.

Important Note: The 6 computer adaptive online exams included with the purchase of this book are the SAME exams that you receive upon purchasing ANY book in the Manhattan GMAT Complete Strategy Guide Set.

⊛ *Fractions, Decimals, & Percents* Online Question Bank

The Bonus Online Question Bank for *Fractions, Decimals, & Percents* consists of 25 extra practice questions (with detailed explanations) that test the variety of concepts and skills covered in this book. These questions provide you with extra practice beyond the problem sets contained in this book. You may use our online timer to practice your pacing by setting time limits for each question in the bank.

⊛ Online Updates to the Contents in this Book

The content presented in this book is updated periodically to ensure that it reflects the GMAT's most current trends. You may view all updates, including any known errors or changes, upon registering for online access.

TABLE *of* CONTENTS

1. Digits & Decimals   11
Problem Set   21

2. Fractions   25
Problem Set   37

3. Percents   41
Problem Set   51

4. Ratios   61
Problem Set   69

5. FDPs   73
Problem Set   79

6. FDP Strategies   83
Problem Set   99

7. Extra FDPs   107
Problem Set   119

Appendix A: Official Guide Problem Sets   125

guide **1**

Chapter 1
of
Fractions, Decimals, & Percents

Digits & Decimals

In This Chapter...

Digits

Decimals

Place Value

Rounding to the Nearest Place Value

Adding Zeroes to Decimals

Powers of 10: Shifting the Decimal

Decimal Operations

Chapter 1:

Digits & Decimals

Digits

Every number is composed of digits. There are only ten digits in our number system: 0, 1, 2, 3, 4, 5, 6, 7, 8, 9. The term digit refers to one building block of a number; it does not refer to a number itself. For example, 356 is a number composed of three digits: 3, 5, and 6.

Integers can be classified by the number of digits they contain. For example:

> 2, 7, and −8 are each single-digit numbers (they are each composed of one digit).
> 43, 63, and −14 are each double-digit numbers (composed of two digits).
> 500,000 and −468,024 are each six-digit numbers (composed of six digits).
> 789,526,622 is a nine-digit number (composed of nine digits).

Non-integers are not generally classified by the number of digits they contain, since you can always add any number of zeroes at the end, on the right side of the decimal point:

> $9.1 = 9.10 = 9.100$

Decimals

GMAT math goes beyond an understanding of the properties of integers (which include the counting numbers, such as 1, 2, 3, and their negative counterparts, such as −1, −2, −3, and 0). The GMAT also tests your ability to understand the numbers that fall in between the integers. Such numbers can be expressed as decimals. For example, the decimal 6.3 falls between the integers 6 and 7:

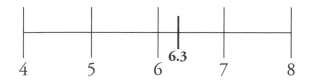

1

Some other examples of decimals include:

Decimals less than −1:   −3.65, −12.01, −145.9
Decimals between −1 and 0:   −0.65, −0.8912, −0.076
Decimals between 0 and 1:   0.65, 0.8912, 0.076
Decimals greater than 1:   3.65, 12.01, 145.9

Note that an integer can be expressed as a decimal by adding the decimal point and the digit 0. For example:

$$8 = 8.0 \qquad\qquad -123 = -123.0 \qquad\qquad 400 = 400.0$$

Place Value

Every digit in a number has a particular place value depending on its location within the number. For example, in the number 452, the digit 2 is in the ones (or "units") place, the digit 5 is in the tens place, and the digit 4 is in the hundreds place. The name of each location corresponds to the "value" of that place. Thus:

2 is worth two "units" (two "ones"), or 2 (= 2 × 1);
5 is worth five tens, or
50 (= 5 × 10); and
4 is worth four hundreds, or 400 (= 4 × 100).

You can now write the number 452 as the **sum** of these products:

$$452 = 4 \times 100 + 5 \times 10 + 2 \times 1$$

6	9	2	5	6	7	8	9	1	0	2	3	.	8	3	4	7
HUNDRED	TEN	ONE	HUNDRED	TEN	ONE	HUNDRED	TEN		HUNDRED	TENS	UNITS OR ONES		TENTHS	HUNDREDTHS	THOUSANDTHS	TEN
BILLIONS	BILLIONS	BILLIONS	MILLIONS	MILLIONS	MILLIONS	THOUSANDS	THOUSANDS	THOUSANDS	REDS							THOUSANDTHS

The chart to the left analyzes the place value of all the digits in the number **692,567,891,023.8347**.

Notice that the place values to the left of the decimal all end in "-s," while the place values to the right of the decimal all end in "-ths." This is because the suffix "-ths" gives these places (to the right of the decimal) a fractional value.

Analyze the end of the preceding number: **0.8347**:

8 is in the tenths place, giving it a value of 8 tenths, or $\dfrac{8}{10}$.

3 is in the hundredths place, giving it a value of 3 hundredths, or $\dfrac{3}{100}$.

4 is in the thousandths place, giving it a value of 4 thousandths, or $\dfrac{4}{1,000}$.

7 is in the ten thousandths place, giving it a value of 7 ten thousandths, or $\dfrac{7}{10,000}$.

To use a concrete example, 0.8 might mean eight tenths of one dollar, which would be 8 dimes or 80 cents. Additionally, 0.03 might mean three hundredths of one dollar, which would be 3 pennies or 3 cents.

Rounding to the Nearest Place Value

The GMAT occasionally requires you to round a number to a specific place value.

> **What is 3.681 rounded to the nearest tenth?**

First, find the digit located in the specified place value. The digit 6 is in the tenths place.

Second, look at the right-digit-neighbor (the digit immediately to the right) of the digit in question. In this case, 8 is the right-digit-neighbor of 6. If the right-digit-neighbor is 5 or greater, round the digit in question UP. Otherwise, leave the digit alone. In this case, since 8 is greater than 5 the digit in question (6) must be rounded up to 7. Thus, 3.681 rounded to the nearest tenth equals 3.7. Note that all the digits to the right of the right-digit-neighbor are irrelevant when rounding.

Rounding appears on the GMAT in the form of questions such as this:

> **If x is the decimal 8.1d5, with d as an unknown digit, and x rounded to the nearest tenth is equal to 8.1, which digits could not be the value of d?**

In order for x to be 8.1 when rounded to the nearest tenth, the right-digit-neighbor, d, must be less than 5. Therefore, d cannot be 5, 6, 7, 8 or 9.

Adding Zeroes to Decimals

Adding zeroes to the end of a decimal or taking zeroes away from the end of a decimal does not change the value of the decimal. For example:

$$3.6 = 3.60 = 3.6000$$

Be careful, however, not to add or remove any zeroes from within a number. Doing so will change the value of the number:

$$7.01 \neq 7.1$$

Powers of 10: Shifting the Decimal

Place values continually decrease from left to right by powers of 10. Understanding this can help you understand the following shortcuts for multiplication and division.

In words	thousands	hundreds	tens	ones	tenths	hundredths	thousandths
In numbers	1,000	100	10	1	0.1	0.01	0.001
In powers of ten	10^3	10^2	10^1	10^0	10^{-1}	10^{-2}	10^{-3}

When you multiply any number by a positive power of 10, move the decimal to the right the specified number of places. This makes positive numbers larger:

$3.9742 \times 10^3 = 3,974.2$ Move the decimal to the right right 3 spaces.
$89.507 \times 10 = 895.07$ Move the decimal to the right 1 space.

When you divide any number by a positive power of 10, move the decimal to the left the specified number of places. This makes positive numbers smaller:

$4,169.2 \div 10^2 = 41.692$ Move the decimal to the left 2 spaces.
$89.507 \div 10 = 8.9507$ Move the decimal to the left 1 space.

Note that if you need to add zeroes in order to shift a decimal, you should do so:

$2.57 \times 10^6 = 2,570,000$ Add 4 zeroes at the end.
$14.29 \div 10^5 = 0.0001429$ Add 3 zeroes at the beginning.

Finally, note that negative powers of 10 reverse the regular process:

$6,782.01 \times 10^{-3} = 6.78201$ $53.0447 \div 10^{-2} = 5,304.47$

You can think about these processes as **trading decimal places for powers of 10**.

MANHATTAN
GMAT

1

For instance, all of the following numbers equal 110,700:

110.7	$\times$	10^3
11.07	$\times$	10^4
1.107	$\times$	10^5
0.1107	$\times$	10^6
0.01107	$\times$	10^7

The first number gets smaller by a factor of 10 as you move the decimal one place to the left, but the second number gets bigger by a factor of 10 to compensate.

Decimal Operations

Addition & Subtraction

To add or subtract decimals, make sure to line up the decimal points. Then add zeroes to make the right sides of the decimals the same length:

4.319 + 221.8

Line up the decimal points and add zeroes.

$$\begin{array}{r} 4.319 \\ + \ 221.800 \\ \hline 226.119 \end{array}$$

10 − 0.063

Line up the decimal points and add zeroes.

$$\begin{array}{r} 10.000 \\ - \ \ 0.063 \\ \hline 9.937 \end{array}$$

Addition and subtraction: Line up the decimal points!

Multiplication

To multiply decimals, ignore the decimal point until the end. Just multiply the numbers as you would if they were whole numbers. Then count the total number of digits to the right of the decimal point in the factors. The product should have the same number of digits to the right of the decimal point.

0.02 × 1.4

Multiply normally:

$$\begin{array}{r} 14 \\ \times \ \ 2 \\ \hline 28 \end{array}$$

There are 3 digits to the right of the decimal point in the factors (0 and 2 in the first factor and 4 in the second factor). Therefore, move the decimal point 3 places to the left in the product: 28 $\longrightarrow$ 0.028.

Multiplication: In the factors, count all the digits to the right of the decimal point—then put that many digits to the right of the decimal point in the product.

If the product ends with 0, count it in this process: $0.8 \times 0.5 = 0.40$, since $8 \times 5 = 40$.

1

If you are multiplying a very large number and a very small number, the following trick works to simplify the calculation: move the decimals **in the opposite direction** the same number of places.

$$0.0003 \times 40{,}000 = ?$$

Move the decimal point **right** four places on the 0.0003 $\longrightarrow$ 3
Move the decimal point **left** four places on the 40,000 $\longrightarrow$ 4

$$0.0003 \times 40{,}000 = 3 \times 4 = 12$$

The reason this technique works is that you are multiplying and then dividing by the same power of 10. In other words, you are **trading decimal places** in one number for decimal places in another number. This is just like trading decimal places for powers of 10, as you saw earlier.

Division

If there is a decimal point in the dividend (the inner number) only, you can simply bring the decimal point straight up to the answer and divide normally:

$$\mathbf{12.42 \div 3} = 4.14$$

$$
\begin{array}{r}
4.14 \\
3\overline{)12.42} \\
\underline{12} \\
04 \\
\underline{3} \\
12
\end{array}
$$

However, if there is a decimal point in the divisor (the outer number), you should shift the decimal point in both the divisor and the dividend to make the *divisor* a whole number. Then, bring the decimal point up and divide:

$$\mathbf{12.42 \div 0.3} \longrightarrow 124.2 \div 3 = 41.4$$

$$
\begin{array}{r}
41.4 \\
3\overline{)124.2} \\
\underline{12} \\
04 \\
\underline{3} \\
12
\end{array}
$$

Move the decimal one space to the right to make 0.3 a whole number. Then, move the decimal one space to the right in 12.42 to make it 124.2.

Division: Divide by whole numbers!

You can always simplify division problems that involve decimals by shifting the decimal point **in the same direction** in both the divisor and the dividend, even when the division problem is expressed as a fraction:

$$\frac{0.0045}{0.09} = \frac{45}{900}$$
Move the decimal 4 spaces to the right to make both the numerator and the denominator whole numbers.

Note that this is essentially the same process as simplifying a fraction. You are simply multiplying the numerator and denominator of the fraction by a power of 10—in this case, 10^4, or 10,000.

Keep track of how you move the decimal point! To simplify multiplication, you can move decimals in opposite directions. But to simplify division, you move decimals in the same direction.

Equivalently, by adding zeroes, you can express the numerator and the denominator as the same units, then simplify:

$$\frac{0.0045}{0.09} = \frac{45}{900} = 45 \text{ ten thousandths} \div 900 \text{ ten thousandths} = \frac{45}{900} = \frac{5}{100} = 0.05$$

Powers and Roots

To square or cube a decimal, you can always simply multiply it by itself once or twice. However, to raise a decimal to a larger power, you can rewrite the decimal as the product of an integer and a power of 10, and then apply the exponent:

$$(0.5)^4 = ?$$

$0.5 = 5 \times 10^{-1}$	Rewrite the decimal.
$(5 \times 10^{-1})^4 = 5^4 \times 10^{-4}$	Apply the exponent to each part.
$5^4 = 25^2 = 625$	Compute the first part and combine.
$625 \times 10^{-4} = 0.0625$	

Solve for roots of decimals the same way. Recall that a root is a number raised to a fractional power: a square root is a number raised to the 1/2 power, a cube root is a number raised to the 1/3 power, etc.:

$$\sqrt[3]{0.000027} = ?$$

Rewrite the decimal. Make the first number something you can take the cube root of easily:

$$0.000027 = 27 \times 10^{-6}$$

$(0.000027)^{1/3} = (27 \times 10^{-6})^{1/3}$	Write the root as a fractional exponent.
$(27)^{1/3} \times (10^{-6})^{1/3} = (27)^{1/3} \times 10^{-2}$	Apply the exponent to each part.
$(27)^{1/3} = 3$ (since $3^3 = 27$)	Compute the first part and combine.
$3 \times 10^{-2} = 0.03$	

1

Powers and roots: Rewrite the decimal using powers of 10!

Once you understand the principles, you can take a shortcut by counting decimal places. For instance, the number of decimal places in the result of a cubed decimal is 3 times the number of decimal places in the original decimal:

$$(0.04)^3 = 0.000064 \qquad (0.04)^3 \qquad = 0.000064$$

2 places   *2 × 3 = 6 places*

Likewise, the number of decimal places in a cube root is 1/3 the number of decimal places in the original decimal:

$$\sqrt[3]{0.000000008} = 0.002 \qquad \sqrt[3]{0.000000008} \qquad = 0.002$$

9 places   *9 ÷ 3 = 3 places*

However, make sure that you can work with powers of 10 using exponent rules.

Problem Set

P

Solve each problem, applying the concepts and rules you learned in this section.

1. In the decimal, 2.4*d*7, *d* represents a digit from 0 to 9. If the value of the decimal rounded to the nearest tenth is less than 2.5, what are the possible values of *d*?

    5 > d

2. If *k* is an integer, and if 0.02468×10^k is greater than 10,000, what is the least possible value of *k*?

    24680

    6

3. Which integer values of *b* would give the number $2002 \div 10^{-b}$ a value between 1 and 100?

    2, 3

4. Simplify: $(4 \times 10^{-2}) - (2.5 \times 10^{-3})$

    0.04 − 0.0025 = 0.0375

5. What is $4,563,021 \div 10^5$, rounded to the nearest whole number?

    46

6. Which integer values of *j* would give the number $-37,129 \times 10^j$ a value between −100 and −1?

    −3, −4

7. Simplify: $\dfrac{0.00081}{0.09}$

    0.009

8. Simplify: $\sqrt[8]{0.00000256}$

    0.2

Solutions

1. **{0, 1, 2, 3, 4}:** If d is 5 or greater, the decimal rounded to the nearest tenth will be 2.5.

2. **6:** Multiplying 0.02468 by a positive power of 10 will shift the decimal point to the right. Simply shift the decimal point to the right until the result is greater than 10,000. Keep track of how many times you shift the decimal point. Shifting the decimal point 5 times results in 2,468. This is still less than 10,000. Shifting one more place yields 24,680, which is greater than 10,000.

3. **{−2, −3}:** In order to give 2002 a value between 1 and 100, you must shift the decimal point to change the number to 2.002 or 20.02. This requires a shift of either two or three places to the left. Remember that, while multiplication shifts the decimal point to the right, division shifts it to the left. To shift the decimal point 2 places to the left, you would divide by 10^2. To shift it 3 places to the left, you would divide by 10^3. Therefore, the exponent $-b = \{2, 3\}$, and $b = \{-2, -3\}$.

4. **0.0375:** First, rewrite the numbers in standard notation by shifting the decimal point. Then, add zeroes, line up the decimal points, and subtract:

$$\begin{array}{r} 0.0400 \\ -\ 0.0025 \\ \hline 0.0375 \end{array}$$

5. **46:** To divide by a positive power of 10, shift the decimal point to the left. This yields 45.63021. To round to the nearest whole number, look at the tenths place. The digit in the tenths place, 6, is more than five. Therefore, the number is closest to 46.

6. **{−3, −4}:** In order to give −37,129 a value between −100 and −1, you must shift the decimal point to change the number to −37.129 or −3.7129. This requires a shift of either three or four places to the left. Remember that multiplication by a positive power of 10 shifts the decimal point to the right. To shift the decimal point 3 places to the left, you would multiply by 10^{-3}. To shift it 4 places to the left, you would multiply by 10^{-4}. Therefore, the exponent $j = \{-3, -4\}$.

7. **0.009:** Shift the decimal point 2 spaces to eliminate the decimal point in the denominator:

$$\frac{0.00081}{0.09} = \frac{0.081}{9}$$

Then divide. First, drop the 3 decimal places: $81 \div 9 = 9$. Then put the 3 decimal places back: 0.009.

8. **0.2:** Write the expression as a decimal raised to a fractional power, using powers of 10 to separate the base from the exponent: $(0.00000256)^{1/8} = (256)^{1/8} \times (10^{-8})^{1/8}$. Next, compute each component separately and combine them at the finish: $(256)^{1/8} \times (10^{-8})^{1/8} = 2 \times 10^{-1} = 0.2$.

Chapter 2 of

Fractions, Decimals, & Percents

Fractions

In This Chapter...

Numerator and Denominator Rules

Simplifying Fractions

Converting Improper Fractions to Mixed Numbers

The Multiplication Shortcut

No Addition or Subtraction Shortcuts

Dividing Fractions: Use the Reciprocal

Division in Disguise

Comparing Fractions: Cross-Multiply

Never Split the Denominator

Chapter 2:

Fractions

Decimals are one way of expressing the numbers that fall in between the integers. Another way of expressing these numbers is fractions.

For example, the fraction $\frac{13}{2}$, which equals 6.5, falls between the integers 6 and 7:

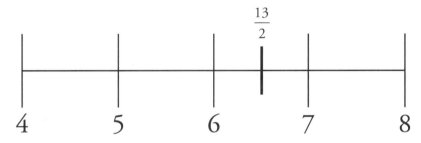

Proper fractions are those that fall between 0 and 1. In proper fractions, the numerator is always smaller than the denominator. For example:

$$\frac{1}{4}, \frac{1}{2}, \frac{2}{3}, \frac{7}{10}$$

Improper fractions are those that are greater than 1. In improper fractions, the numerator is greater than the denominator. For example:

$$\frac{5}{4}, \frac{13}{2}, \frac{11}{3}, \frac{101}{10}$$

Improper fractions can be rewritten as **mixed numbers**. A mixed number is an integer and a proper fraction. For example:

$$\frac{5}{4}=1\frac{1}{4} \qquad \frac{13}{2}=6\frac{1}{2} \qquad \frac{11}{3}=3\frac{2}{3} \qquad \frac{101}{10}=10\frac{1}{10}$$

Although the preceding examples use positive fractions, note that fractions and mixed numbers can be negative as well.

Numerator and Denominator Rules

Certain key rules govern the relationship between the numerator (the top number) and the denominator (the bottom number) of proper fractions. These rules are important to internalize, but keep in mind that, as written, they **only apply to positive fractions**.

As the **numerator** goes up, the fraction **increases**. If you increase the numerator of a fraction, while holding the denominator constant, the fraction increases in value:

$$\frac{1}{8}<\frac{2}{8}<\frac{3}{8}<\frac{4}{8}<\frac{5}{8}<\frac{6}{8}<\frac{7}{8}<\frac{8}{8}<\frac{9}{8}<\frac{10}{8}<\ldots$$

As the **denominator** goes up, the fraction **decreases**. If you increase the denominator of a fraction, while holding the numerator constant, the fraction decreases in value as it approaches 0:

$$\frac{3}{2}>\frac{3}{3}>\frac{3}{4}>\frac{3}{5}>\frac{3}{6}\ldots>\frac{3}{1,000}\ldots\rightarrow 0$$

Adding the same number to **both** the numerator and the denominator brings the fraction **closer** to 1, regardless of the fraction's value.

If the fraction is originally smaller than 1, the fraction **increases** in value as it approaches 1:

$$\frac{1}{2}<\frac{1+1}{2+1}=\frac{2}{3}<\frac{2+9}{3+9}=\frac{11}{12}<\frac{11+1,000}{12+1,000}=\frac{1,011}{1,012}$$

Thus: $\qquad \dfrac{1}{2}<\dfrac{2}{3}<\dfrac{11}{12}<\dfrac{1,011}{1,012}\ldots\rightarrow 1$

Conversely, if the fraction is originally larger than 1, the fraction **decreases** in value as it approaches 1:

$$\frac{3}{2}>\frac{3+1}{2+1}=\frac{4}{3}>\frac{4+9}{3+9}=\frac{13}{12}>\frac{13+1,000}{12+1,000}=\frac{1,013}{1,012}$$

Thus: $\qquad \dfrac{3}{2}>\dfrac{4}{3}>\dfrac{13}{12}>\dfrac{1,013}{1,012}\ldots\rightarrow 1$

Simplifying Fractions

Simplifying fractions is a process that attempts to express a fraction in its lowest terms. Fractional answers on the GMAT will always be presented in fully simplified form. The process of simplifying is governed by one simple rule: **multiplying** or **dividing** both the numerator and the denominator by the same number does not change the value of the fraction.

$$\frac{4}{5} = \frac{4(3)}{5(3)} = \frac{12}{15} = \frac{12(2)}{15(2)} = \frac{24}{30} \qquad\qquad \frac{24}{30} = \frac{24 \div 6}{30 \div 6} = \frac{4}{5}$$

Simplifying a fraction means dividing both the numerator and the denominator by a common factor. This must be repeated until no common factors remain:

$$\frac{40}{30} = \frac{40 \div 5}{30 \div 5} = \frac{8}{6} = \frac{8 \div 2}{6 \div 2} = \frac{4}{3} \qquad \text{or in one step:} \qquad \frac{40}{30} = \frac{40 \div 10}{30 \div 10} = \frac{4}{3}$$

Converting Improper Fractions to Mixed Numbers

To convert an improper fraction into a mixed number, simply divide the numerator by the denominator, stopping when you reach a remainder smaller than the denominator:

$$\frac{9}{4} = 9 \div 4 = 4\overline{)9} \;\begin{array}{r} 2 \\ \underline{8} \\ 1 \end{array}$$

Since $9 \div 4 = 2$ with a remainder of 1, you can write the improper fraction as the integer 2 with a fractional part of 1 over the original denominator of 4.

Thus, $\frac{9}{4} = 2\frac{1}{4}$.

This process can also work in reverse. In order to convert a mixed number into an improper fraction (something you need to do in order to multiply or divide mixed numbers), use the following procedure:

$2\frac{1}{4}$ Multiply the whole number (2) by the denominator (4) and add the numerator (1).

$2 \times 4 + 1 = 9$ Now place the number 9 over the original denominator, 4: $\frac{9}{4}$.

Alternatively, since $2\frac{1}{4} = 2 + \frac{1}{4}$, just split the mixed fraction into its two parts and rewrite the whole number using a common denominator:

$$2\frac{1}{4} = 2 + \frac{1}{4} = \frac{8}{4} + \frac{1}{4} = \frac{9}{4}$$

The Multiplication Shortcut

You could first multiply the numerators together, then multiply the denominators together, and finally simplify the resulting product. For example:

$$\frac{8}{15}\times\frac{35}{72}=\frac{8(35)}{15(72)}=\frac{280}{1{,}080}=\frac{28}{108}=\frac{7}{27}$$

There is, however, a shortcut that can make fraction multiplication much less tedious. The shortcut is to simplify your products multiplying. This is also known as "cancelling."

Notice that the **8** in the numerator and the **72** in the denominator both have 8 as a factor. Thus, they can be simplified from $\frac{8}{72}$ to $\frac{1}{9}$.

Notice also that **35** in the numerator and **15** in the denominator both have 5 as a factor. Thus, they can be simplified from $\frac{35}{15}$ to $\frac{7}{3}$.

Now the multiplication will be easier and no further simplification will be necessary:

$$\frac{8}{15}\times\frac{35}{72}=\frac{8(35)}{15(72)}=\frac{1(7)}{3(9)}=\frac{7}{27}$$

Always try to cancel factors before multiplying fractions!

In order to multiply mixed numbers, you should first convert each mixed number into an improper fraction:

$$2\frac{1}{3}\times6\frac{3}{5}=\frac{7}{3}\times\frac{33}{5}$$

You can simplify the problem, using the multiplication shortcut of cancelling, and then convert the result to a mixed number:

$$\frac{7}{3}\times\frac{33}{5}=\frac{7(33)}{3(5)}=\frac{7(11)}{1(5)}=\frac{77}{5}=15\frac{2}{5}$$

MANHATTAN
GMAT

No Addition or Subtraction Shortcuts

While shortcuts are very useful when multiplying fractions, you must be careful **not** to take any short-cuts when adding or subtracting fractions. In order to add or subtract fractions, you must

1. find a common denominator,
2. change each fraction so that it is expressed using this common denominator, and
3. add up the numerators only.

You may need to simplify the result when you are finished; the resulting fraction may not be in reduced form:

$$\frac{3}{8} + \frac{7}{12}$$

A common denominator is 24. Thus, $\frac{3}{8} = \frac{9}{24}$ and $\frac{7}{12} = \frac{14}{24}$.

$$\frac{9}{24} + \frac{14}{24}$$

Express each fraction using the common denominator 24.

$$\frac{9}{24} + \frac{14}{24} = \frac{23}{24}$$

Finally, add the numerators to find the answer.

Another example:

$$\frac{11}{15} - \frac{7}{30}$$

A common denominator is 30. $\frac{11}{15} = \frac{22}{30}$ and $\frac{7}{30}$ stays the same.

$$\frac{22}{30} - \frac{7}{30}$$

Express each fraction using the common denominator 30.

$$\frac{22}{30} - \frac{7}{30} = \frac{15}{30}$$

Subtract the numerators.

$$\frac{15}{30} = \frac{1}{2}$$

Simplify $\frac{15}{30}$ to find the answer: $\frac{1}{2}$.

In order to add or subtract mixed numbers, you can convert to improper fractions, or you can set up the problem vertically and solve the fraction first and the whole number last:

Addition	**Subtraction**	You may wind up with a

$$
\begin{array}{l}
7\frac{1}{3} = 7\frac{2}{6} \\[2mm]
+\ 4\frac{1}{2} = 4\frac{3}{6} \\[1mm]
\hline
\qquad 11\frac{5}{6}
\end{array}
\qquad
\begin{array}{l}
7\frac{1}{3} = 7\frac{2}{6} = 7 + \frac{2}{6} \\[2mm]
-\ 4\frac{1}{2} = 4\frac{3}{6} = 4 + \frac{3}{6} \\[1mm]
\hline
3 + \frac{-1}{6} = 2 + \frac{5}{6} = 2\frac{5}{6}
\end{array}
$$

You may wind up with a negative fraction. Simply combine it afterwards with the whole number as shown below.

Dividing Fractions: Use the Reciprocal

In order to divide fractions, you must first understand the concept of the reciprocal. You can think of the reciprocal as the fraction flipped upside down:

The reciprocal of $\dfrac{3}{4}$ is $\dfrac{4}{3}$.   The reciprocal of $\dfrac{2}{9}$ is $\dfrac{9}{2}$.

What is the reciprocal of an integer? Think of an integer as a fraction with a denominator of 1. Thus, the integer 5 is really just $\dfrac{5}{1}$. To find the reciprocal, just flip it:

The reciprocal of **5**, or $\dfrac{5}{1}$, is $\dfrac{1}{5}$.   The reciprocal of **8** is $\dfrac{1}{8}$.

To check if you have found the reciprocal of a number, use this rule: **The product of a number and its reciprocal always equals 1.** The following examples reveal this to be true:

$$\frac{3}{4}\times\frac{4}{3}=\frac{12}{12}=1 \qquad 5\times\frac{1}{5}=\frac{5}{1}\times\frac{1}{5}=\frac{5}{5}=1 \qquad \sqrt{7}\times\frac{\sqrt{7}}{7}=\frac{\sqrt{7}}{1}\times\frac{\sqrt{7}}{7}=\frac{7}{7}=1$$

In order to divide fractions,

    (1)   change the divisor into its reciprocal, and then

    (2)   multiply the fractions. Note that the divisor is the second number:

$\dfrac{1}{2}\div\dfrac{3}{4}$ First, change the divisor $\dfrac{3}{4}$ into its reciprocal $\dfrac{4}{3}$.

$\dfrac{1}{2}\times\dfrac{4}{3}=\dfrac{2}{3}$ Then, multiply the fractions and simplify to lowest terms.

In order to divide mixed numbers, first change them into improper fractions:

$5\dfrac{2}{3}\div8\dfrac{1}{2}=\dfrac{17}{3}\div\dfrac{17}{2}$ Then, change the divisor $\dfrac{17}{2}$ into its reciprocal $\dfrac{2}{17}$.

$\dfrac{17}{3}\times\dfrac{2}{17}=\dfrac{2}{3}$ Multiply the fractions, cancelling where you can.

Division in Disguise

Sometimes, dividing fractions can be written in a confusing way. Consider one of the previous examples:

$\dfrac{1}{2} \div \dfrac{3}{4}$ can also be written as a "double-decker" fraction this way: $\dfrac{\dfrac{1}{2}}{\dfrac{3}{4}}$

Do not be confused. You can rewrite this as the top fraction divided by the bottom fraction, and solve it normally (by using the reciprocal of the bottom fraction and then multiplying):

$$\dfrac{\dfrac{1}{2}}{\dfrac{3}{4}} = \dfrac{1}{2} \div \dfrac{3}{4} = \dfrac{1}{2} \times \dfrac{4}{3} = \dfrac{2}{3}$$

Also notice that you can often simplify quickly by multiplying both top and bottom by a common denominator:

$$\dfrac{\dfrac{1}{2}}{\dfrac{3}{4}} = \dfrac{\dfrac{1}{2} \times 4}{\dfrac{3}{4} \times 4} = \dfrac{2}{3}$$

Comparing Fractions: Cross-Multiply

Which fraction is greater, $\dfrac{7}{9}$ or $\dfrac{4}{5}$?

The traditional method of comparing fractions involves finding a common denominator and comparing the two fractions. The common denominator of 9 and 5 is 45.

Thus, $\dfrac{7}{9} = \dfrac{35}{45}$ and $\dfrac{4}{5} = \dfrac{36}{45}$. You can see that $\dfrac{4}{5}$ is slightly bigger than $\dfrac{7}{9}$.

However, there is a shortcut to comparing fractions called cross-multiplication. This is a process that involves multiplying the numerator of one fraction with the denominator of the other fraction, and vice versa:

$(7 \times 5) = 35 \qquad (4 \times 9) = 36$

$\dfrac{7}{9} \quad\overset{\displaystyle\longleftarrow}{\underset{\displaystyle\longrightarrow}{\times}}\quad \dfrac{4}{5}$ Set up the fractions next to each other.

Cross-multiply the fractions and put each answer by the corresponding **numerator** (*not* the denominator!)

$$\frac{7}{9} \quad < \quad \frac{4}{5}$$

Since 35 is less than 36, the first fraction must be less than the second one.

This process can save you a lot of time when comparing fractions (usually more than two!) on the GMAT.

Never Split the Denominator

One final rule, perhaps the most important one, is one that you must always remember when working with complex fractions. A complex fraction is a fraction in which there is a sum or a difference in the numerator or the denominator. Three examples of complex fractions are:

(a) $\dfrac{15+10}{5}$ (b) $\dfrac{5}{15+10}$ (c) $\dfrac{15+10}{5+2}$

In example (a), the numerator is expressed as a sum.
In example (b), the denominator is expressed as a sum.
In example (c), both the numerator and the denominator are expressed as sums.

When simplifying fractions that incorporate sums or differences, remember this rule: You may split up the terms of the numerator, but you may **never** split the terms of the **denominator**.

Thus, the terms in example (a) may be split:

$$\frac{15+10}{5} = \frac{15}{5} + \frac{10}{5} = 3 + 2 = 5$$

But the terms in example (b) may not be split:

$$\frac{5}{15+10} \neq \frac{5}{15} + \frac{5}{10} \quad \textbf{NO!}$$

Instead, simplify the denominator first:

$$\frac{5}{15+10} = \frac{5}{25} = \frac{1}{5}$$

The terms in example (c) may not be split either:

$$\frac{15+10}{5+2} \neq \frac{15}{5} + \frac{10}{2} \quad \textbf{NO!}$$

Instead, simplify both parts of the fraction:

MANHATTAN
GMAT

$$\frac{15+10}{5+2}=\frac{25}{7}=3\frac{4}{7}$$

Often, GMAT problems will involve complex fractions with variables. On these problems, it is tempting to split the denominator. Do not fall for it!

It is tempting to perform the following simplification:

$$\frac{5x-2y}{x-y}=\frac{5x}{x}-\frac{2y}{y}=5-2=3$$

But this is **wrong** because you cannot split terms in the denominator.

The reality is that $\dfrac{5x-2y}{x-y}$ cannot be simplified further.

On the other hand, the expression $\dfrac{6x-15y}{10}$ can be simplified by splitting the difference, because this difference appears in the numerator:

Thus: $\dfrac{6x-15y}{10}=\dfrac{6x}{10}-\dfrac{15y}{10}=\dfrac{3x}{5}-\dfrac{3y}{2}$

✱ cannot split denominators

✱ product of fraction & its reciprocal = 1

Problem Set

For problems 1–5, decide whether the given operation will yield an **increase**, a **decrease**, or a result that will **stay the same**.

1. Multiply the numerator of a positive, proper fraction by $\frac{3}{2}$. ↑

2. Add 1 to the numerator of a positive, proper fraction and subtract 1 from its denominator. ↑

    $\frac{2}{3} - \frac{3}{2}$

3. Multiply both the numerator and denominator of a positive, proper fraction by $3\frac{1}{2}$. $\frac{7}{2} \times \frac{1}{2}$ $\frac{7}{4}$

    ↛ stay same

4. Multiply a positive, proper fraction by $\frac{3}{8}$.   ↓ $1\frac{3}{4}$

5. Divide a positive, proper fraction by $\frac{3}{13}$.   ↑ $\frac{1}{2} \times \frac{13}{3} = \frac{13}{6}$

Solve problems 6–15.

cannot split denominator

6. Simplify: $\frac{10x}{5+x}$

7. Simplify: $\frac{8(3)(x)^2(3)}{6x}$ $24x^2$ $\frac{72x^2}{6x}$ $\frac{72^2}{6x}$ → $6x\sqrt{12x}$ $=12x$

8. Simplify: $\dfrac{\frac{3}{5}+\frac{1}{3}}{\frac{2}{3}+\frac{2}{5}}$ $\dfrac{\frac{9+5}{15}}{\frac{10+6}{15}}$ $\frac{14}{15} \times \frac{15}{16} = \frac{14}{16}$

9. Simplify: $\frac{12ab^3 - 6a^2b}{3ab}$ (given that $ab \neq 0$) $= 4b^2 - 2a = 2(2b^2 - a)$

10. Are $\left(\frac{\sqrt{3}}{2}\right)$ and $\left(\frac{2\sqrt{3}}{3}\right)$ reciprocals? $\sqrt{3}$ $\cancel{3}$ Yes

    $= \frac{3}{2\sqrt{3}}$ No

    $\frac{3}{2}$ $\frac{2(3)}{3} = \frac{6}{3} = 2$

Solutions

1. **Increase:** Multiplying the numerator of a positive fraction increases the numerator. As the numerator of a positive, proper fraction increases, its value increases.

2. **Increase:** As the numerator of a positive, proper fraction increases, the value of the fraction increases. As the denominator of a positive, proper fraction decreases, the value of the fraction also increases. Both actions will work to increase the value of the fraction.

3. **Stay the same:** Multiplying or dividing the numerator and denominator of a fraction by the same number will not change the value of the fraction.

4. **Decrease:** Multiplying a positive number by a proper fraction decreases the number.

5. **Increase:** Dividing a positive number by a positive, proper fraction increases the number.

6. **Cannot simplify:** There is no way to simplify this fraction; it is already in simplest form. Remember, you cannot split the denominator!

7. **12x:** First, cancel terms in both the numerator and the denominator. Then combine terms:

$$\frac{8(3)(x)^2(3)}{6x} = \frac{8(3)(x)^2(3)}{6\,2x} = \frac{8\,4(x)^2(3)}{2x} = \frac{4(x)^2(3)}{x} = 4(x)(3) = 12x$$

8. $\dfrac{7}{8}$ **:** First, add the fractions in the numerator and denominator: $\dfrac{\dfrac{14}{15}}{\dfrac{16}{15}} = \dfrac{14}{15} \times \dfrac{15}{16} = \dfrac{7}{8}$.

Alternately, to save time, multiply each of the small fractions by 15, which is the common denominator of all the fractions in the problem. Because you are multiplying the numerator *and* the denominator of the whole complex fraction by 15, you are not changing its value:

$$\frac{9+5}{10+6} = \frac{14}{16} = \frac{7}{8}$$

9. **2(2b² − a) or 4b² − 2a:** First, factor out common terms in the numerator. Then, cancel terms in both the numerator and denominator:

$$\frac{6ab(2b^2 - a)}{3ab} = 2(2b^2 - a) \text{ or } 4b^2 - 2a$$

10. **Yes:** The product of a number and its reciprocal must equal 1. To test whether or not two numbers are reciprocals, multiply them. If the product is 1, they are reciprocals; if it is not, they are not:

P

$$\frac{\sqrt{3}}{2} \times \frac{2\sqrt{3}}{3} = \frac{2(\sqrt{3})^2}{2(3)} = \frac{6}{6} = 1$$

Thus, the numbers are indeed reciprocals.

Chapter 3
of
Fractions, Decimals, & Percents

Percents

In This Chapter...

Percents as Decimals: Multiplication Shortcut

Percent, Of, Is, What

Percent Increase and Decrease

Percent Change vs. Percent of Original

Successive Percents

Interest Formulas

Chapter 3:

Percents

The other major way to express a part–whole relationship (in addition to decimals and fractions) is to use percents. Percent literally means "per one hundred." One can conceive of percent as simply a special type of fraction or decimal that involves the number 100:

> 75% of the students like chocolate ice cream.

This means that, out of every 100 students, 75 like chocolate ice cream.

In fraction form, you write this as 75/100, which simplifies to 3/4.

In decimal form, you write this as 0.75, or seventy-five hundredths.

One common mistake is the belief that 100% equals 100. This is not correct. In fact, 100% means 100/100, or one hundred hundredths. Therefore, 100% = 1.

Percent problems occur frequently on the GMAT. The key to percent questions is to translate the language of the problem into equations and solve for the desired value.

Percents as Decimals: Multiplication Shortcut

One way of working with percents is by converting them into decimals. Percents can be converted into decimals by moving the decimal point 2 spaces to the left:

525% = 5.25	52.5% = 0.525	5.25% = 0.0525	0.525% = 0.00525

A decimal can be converted into a percentage by moving the decimal point two spaces to the right. For example:

0.6 = 60%	0.28 = 28%	0.459 = 45.9%	1.3 = 130%

Remember, the percentage is always bigger than the decimal!

Percent, Of, Is, What

These four words are by far the most important when translating percent questions. In fact, any percent problem can be rephrased in terms of these four words:

Percent	=	divide by 100	(/100)
Of	=	multiply	(×)
Is	=	equals	(=)
What	=	unknown value	(x)

What is 70 percent of 120 ?

As you read left to right, translate the question directly into an equation:

x	=	70	/100	×	120
What	is	70	percent	of	120?

Now you can solve the equation:

$$x = \frac{70}{100} \times 120$$
$$x = \frac{7}{10} \times 120$$
$$x = 7 \times 12$$
$$x = 84$$

This translation works no matter what order the words appear.

30 is what percent of 50?

This statement can, and should, be translated directly into an equation:

30	=	x	/100	×	50
30	is	what	percent	of	50?

Every time you create one of these equations, your goal is the same: Solve for x.

x represents the unknown value that you have been asked to find. By isolating x, you will answer the question.

You can use this equation to solve for x:

$$30 = \frac{x}{100} \times 50$$
$$30 = \frac{x}{2}$$
$$60 = x$$

Look for these four words as you translate percent problems into equations; they serve as a good clue as to how the equation should be structured.

Percent Increase and Decrease

Consider this example:

> The price of a coffee cup increased from 80 cents to 84 cents. By what percent did the price change?

Whenever you are concerned with a change in a percent, set up this equation:

Original + Change = New

This equation is true for not only the percents involved, but also the actual amounts. Thus:

Original Value	+	Change in Value	=	New Value
80 cents	+	4 cents	=	84 cents

Although you don't know the actual percentages yet, the same relationship applies. Remember that, when dealing with percents, the Original Percent is *always* 100%:

Original Percent	+	Change Percent	=	New Percent
100%	+	?	=	?

There are two important equations to remember that connect the actual values to their corresponding percents.

If you want to find the *change* in percent or *change* in actual value, use the following equation:

$$\textbf{Percent Change} = \frac{\textbf{Change in Value}}{\textbf{Original Value}}$$

If, however, you want to find the new percentage or the new value, use the following equation instead:

$$\text{New Percent} = \frac{\text{New Value}}{\text{Original Value}}$$

In the example above, you want to find the *change* in percent. Use the first equation. The percent change is the value you are looking for, so replace it with *x*. Also, because it is a percent, write *x*/100 to reflect the percentage:

$$\text{Percent Change} = \frac{\text{Change in Value}}{\text{Original Value}}$$

$$\frac{x}{100} = \frac{4}{80}$$

$$80x = 400$$

$$x = 5$$

Therefore, the price has been increased 5%.

Again, these two equations will work no matter how the question is asked. For example:

If the price of a $30 shirt is decreased by 20%, what is the final price of the shirt?

You have been asked for the final price of the shirt, so you want to use the equation that deals with the *new* value:

$$\text{New Percent} = \frac{\text{New Value}}{\text{Original Value}}$$

Notice, though, that the question didn't tell you the new percent, it told us the percent decrease. This is not actually a problem, it just requires one additional step. If the price decreases by 20%, then the new price is 100% − 20% = 80% of the original. Use the new percent, not the decrease in percent, to solve for the new price directly.

Once again, use *x* to represent the value you are solving for, the new price:

$$\frac{80}{100} = \frac{x}{30}$$

$$\frac{4}{5} = \frac{x}{30}$$

$$\frac{4}{1} = \frac{x}{6}$$

$$24 = x$$

The new price of the shirt is $24.

MANHATTAN
GMAT

Percent Change vs. Percent of Original

You could have found 20% of $30 and subtracted it, but it's best to connect percent change problems to the two main equations we've been discussing. Furthermore, in the shirt problem, the step that changed a 20% decrease to 80% of the original may have seemed minor, but it allowed you to do less work and still arrive at the answer.

A percent change can always be rephrased as a percent of the original, and a percent of the original can always be rephrased as a percent change.

Be comfortable switching between the two forms so that you can directly solve for the desired value:

10% increase = 110% of the original	130% of the original = 30% increase
10% greater than = 110% of the original	130% of the original = 30% greater than
45% decrease = 55% of the original	75% of the original = 25% decrease
45% less than = 55% of the original	75% of the original = 25% less than

Remember that "increase" is equivalent to "greater than" and "decrease" is equivalent to "less than."

Use this conversion to save steps on percent problems. For example:

> What number is 50% greater than 60 ?

50% greater than is the same as 150% of. You can rewrite the question:

> What number is 150% of 60 ?

You can translate this question directly into an equation. In this case, it is easier to translate 150% to 1.5, instead of 150/100:

$$x = 1.5 \times 60$$
$$x = 90$$

You can consistently save time on percent problems by calculating directly for the desired number.

Successive Percents

One of the GMAT's favorite tricks involves successive percents. For example:

> If a ticket increased in price by 20%, and then increased again by 5%, by what percent did the ticket price increase in total?

Although it may seem counter-intuitive, the answer is *not* 25%.

Walk through this with real numbers. If the ticket originally cost $100, then the first increase would bring the ticket price up to $120 ($120 is 120% of $100).

The second increase is now based on this new ticket price. The number you need to calculate is 105% of the *new* price, which is $120:

$$1.05 \times 120 = \$126$$

Since the price increased by $26 (from $100 to $126), the overall percent increase is **26%**, not 25%.

Successive percents **cannot** simply be added together. This holds for successive increases, successive decreases, and for combinations of increases and decreases.

In fact, one of the GMAT's favorite successive percents tricks involves an increase and a decrease. For example:

> The cost of a plane ticket is increased by 25%. Later, the ticket goes on sale and the price is reduced 20%. What is the overall percent change in the price of the ticket?

You can answer this question very quickly by lumping the percents into one calculation. A 25% increase followed by a 20% decrease is the same as 125% of 80% of the original number:

$$\left(\frac{125}{100}\right)\left(\frac{80}{100}\right)x =$$

$$\left(\frac{5}{4}\right)\left(\frac{4}{5}\right)x = x$$

The 20% decrease entirely offsets the 25% increase. The new price is exactly the same as the original price.

When you need to calculate successive percents, always rephrase the percents to percent of the original.

Interest Formulas

Certain GMAT problems require a working knowledge of compound interest. The formula looks quite complicated:

$$\textbf{Compound Interest} = P\left(1+\frac{r}{n}\right)^{nt}$$

In this equation, P = principal, r = rate (in decimal form), n = number of times per year, and t = number of years.

A much simpler way of thinking of compound interest is as a successive percents problem:

> A bank account with $200 earns 5% annual interest, compounded annually. If there are no deposits or withdrawals, how much money will the account have after 2 years?

The first thing you need to do is calculate how many times the interest will compound. It compounds once a year for 2 years. It will compound twice.

If the account earns 5% interest, that is an increase of 5% each year. In other words, the new value of the account is 105% of 105% of $200. You can set up an equation and solve:

$$1.05 \times 1.05 \times 200 =$$
$$1.1025 \times 200 = 220.50$$

After two years of interest, there is $220.50 in the account.

If the interest compounds quarterly, the process is the same, although there are a few extra steps. For example:

> A bank account with $100 earns 8% annual interest, compounded quarterly. If there are no deposits or withdrawals. how much money will be in the account after 6 months?

First, you figure out how many times the interest compounds. If the interest compounds quarterly, it compounds every 3 months. In 6 months, the interest will compound twice.

There is one other difference. The 8% interest is spread evenly throughout the year. The interest compounds 4 times each year, so each time it compounds at one-fourth of the total interest.

In other words, each time it compounds, there is a 2% increase. That means that after 6 months, the new value of the account will be 102% of 102% of $100:

$$1.02 \times 1.02 \times 100 =$$
$$1.0404 \times 100 = 104.04$$

After 6 months, there will be $104.04 in the account.

Instead of learning a complicated formula for compound interest, just remember to treat compound interest problems like successive percent problems.

Problem Set

Solve the following problems. Use a percent table to organize percent problems, and pick 100 when dealing with unspecified amounts.

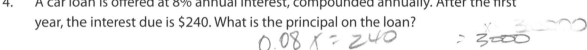

1. $x\%$ of y is 10. $y\%$ of 120 is 48. What is x?

    25%

2. A stereo was marked down by 30% and sold for $84. What was the presale price of the stereo?

    $84 = 0.7x$ *120*

3. If y is decreased by 20% and then increased by 60%, what is the new number, expressed in terms of y?

    1.6 (0.8y)

4. A car loan is offered at 8% annual interest, compounded annually. After the first year, the interest due is $240. What is the principal on the loan?

    $0.08x = 240$ *= 3000*

5. A bowl is half full of water. Four cups of water are then added to the bowl, filling the bowl to 70% of its capacity. How many cups of water are now in the bowl?

    $0.2x = 4$ *$x = 20$*   *→14*

6. x is 40% of y. 50% of y is 40. 16 is what percent of x?

    $\frac{x}{y} = 40$ *$y(0.5) = 40$*   *$\frac{x}{y} = (0.5)$*   *$\frac{x}{y} = \frac{y}{2}$*

7. 800, increased by 50% and then decreased by 30%, yields what number?

    840

8. Lori deposits $10,000 in a savings account at 10% annual interest, compounded annually. After 3 years, what is the balance on the account? (Assume Lori makes no deposits or withdrawals.)

    1200

9. If 1,500 is increased by 20%, and then reduced by $y\%$, yielding 1,080, what is y?

    $36\overline{)2}$

10. A bottle is 80% full. The liquid in the bottle consists of 60% guava juice and 40% pineapple juice. The remainder of the bottle is then filled with 200 mL of rum. How much guava juice is in the bottle?

    10000 @10% 0.1
    11000
    1100
    12100   = 13310

    x=32   16=0.5

    $\frac{x}{y} = \frac{4}{10} = 0.4$ $y(\frac{1}{2})=40$
    $\frac{y}{2} = 40 →$
    32
    $\frac{x}{80} = \frac{4}{10}$ y = 80

Solutions

1. **25:** You can translate both these statements into equations:

$x\%$ of y is 10	→	$x/100 \times y = 10$
$y\%$ of 120 is 48	→	$y/100 \times 120 = 48$

You can use the second equation to solve for y:

$$\frac{y}{100} \times 120 = 48$$

$$\frac{y}{10} \times 12 = 48$$

$$\frac{y}{5} \times 6 = 48$$

$$y = 48 \times \frac{5}{6}$$

$$y = 8 \times \frac{5}{1}$$

$$y = 40$$

Now plug this value for y into the first equation to solve for x:

$$\frac{x}{100} \times 40 = 10$$

$$\frac{x}{5} \times 2 = 10$$

$$x = 10 \times \frac{5}{2}$$

$$x = 5 \times \frac{5}{1}$$

$$x = 25$$

2. **\$120:** You know the new price of the stereo, so you can use the following formula:

$$\text{New Percent} = \frac{\text{New Value}}{\text{Original Value}}$$

The New Value of the stereo is \$84. If the price of the stereo was marked down 30%, then the New Percent is $100 - 30 = 70\%$. Finally, the Original Value is the value you're asked for, so you can replace it with x:

$$\frac{70}{100} = \frac{84}{x}$$

$$\frac{7}{10} = \frac{84}{x}$$

$$7x = 840$$

$$x = 120$$

Alternatively, you could rephrase the given information to say the following:

$84 IS 70% of the original price of the stereo.

You could translate this statement into an equation and solve:

$$84 = \left(\frac{70}{100}\right)x$$

$$84 = \left(\frac{7}{10}\right)x$$

$$840 = 7x$$

$$120 = x$$

3. **1.28y:** If y is decreased by 20% and increased by 60%, that is the same as saying that the new number is 80% of 160% of y. Convert the percents to decimals as you translate and solve:

$$0.8 \times 1.6 \times y = 1.28y$$

4. **$3,000:** Although this looks like an interest problem, you can think of it as a percent change problem. The percent change is 8%, and the change in value is $240:

$$\text{Percent Change} = \frac{\text{Change in Value}}{\text{Original Value}}$$

$$\frac{8}{100} = \frac{240}{x}$$

$$8x = 24,000$$

$$x = 3,000$$

The principal amount of the loan is $3,000.

Alternatively, you could rephrase the given information to say the following:

$240 IS 8% of the total loan.

You could then translate this statement into an equation and solve:

$$240 = \left(\frac{8}{100}\right)x$$
$$24,000 = 8x$$
$$3,000 = x$$

5. **14 cups of water:** If the bowl was already half full of water, then it was originally 50% full. Adding 4 cups of water increased the percentage by 20% of the total capacity of the bowl.

You can use the percent change formula to solve for the total capacity of the bowl:

$$\text{Percent Change} = \frac{\text{Change in Value}}{\text{Original Value}}$$
$$\frac{20}{100} = \frac{4}{x}$$
$$\frac{1}{5} = \frac{4}{x}$$
$$x = 20$$

The total capacity of the bowl is 20 cups, but the question asks for the total number of cups currently in the bowl. You know the bowl is 70% full. You can ask the question, "What is 70% of 20?" and solve:

$$x = \frac{70}{100} \times 20$$
$$x = \frac{7}{10} \times 20$$
$$10x = 140$$
$$x = 14$$

There are 14 cups of water in the bowl.

Alternatively, you can save time by solving directly for 70% rather than by first solving for the full capacity. 4 represents 20% of the capacity. Let x represent 70% of the capacity. Set up a proportion and solve for x:

$$\frac{4}{x} = \frac{20}{70}$$
$$\frac{4}{x} = \frac{2}{7}$$
$$28 = 2x$$
$$14 = x$$

6. **50%:** You can translate the first two sentences directly into equations:

$$x \text{ is } 40\% \text{ of } y \qquad \rightarrow \qquad x = \left(\frac{40}{100}\right)y$$

$$50\% \text{ of } y \text{ is } 40 \qquad \rightarrow \qquad \left(\frac{50}{100}\right)y = 40$$

You can solve the second equation for y:

$$\left(\frac{50}{100}\right)y = 40$$

$$\left(\frac{1}{2}\right)y = 40$$

$$\frac{y}{2} = 40$$

$$y = 80$$

Now you can replace y with 80 in the first equation to solve for x:

$$x = \left(\frac{40}{100}\right)(80)$$

$$x = \frac{4}{10} \times 80$$

$$x = 4 \times 8 = 32$$

Be careful now. The question asks, "16 is what percent of x ?"

You know that $x = 32$, so this question is really asking, "16 is what percent of 32 ?"

Create a new variable (z) to represent the unknown value in the question and solve:

$$16 = \frac{z}{100} \times 32$$

$$16 \times \frac{100}{32} = z$$

$$1 \times \frac{100}{2} = z$$

$$50 = z$$

16 is 50% of x.

7. 840: This is a successive percent question. 800 increased by 50% and decreased by 30% is the same as 150% of 70% of 800:

$$\frac{150}{100} \times \frac{70}{100} \times 800 =$$
$$\frac{3}{2} \times \frac{7}{10} \times 800 =$$
$$\frac{21}{20} \times 800 =$$
$$21 \times 40 = 840$$

P

8. $13,310: Treat this problem as a successive percent. If the interest compounds annually, then it will compound three times in three years.

Each time it compounds, there is a 10% increase in the value of the account. The new value is 110% of 110% of 110% of $10,000.

$$\left(\frac{110}{100}\right)\left(\frac{110}{100}\right)\left(\frac{110}{100}\right)10,000 =$$
$$\left(\frac{11}{10}\right)\left(\frac{11}{10}\right)\left(\frac{11}{10}\right)10,000 =$$
$$(11)(11)(11)10 =$$
$$121 \times 110 = 13,310$$

After three years, there will be $13,310 in the account.

9. 40%: There are a number of ways to answer this question. You can break the question into two parts.

First, 1,500 is increased by 20%. 120% percent of 1,500 is:

$$\left(\frac{120}{100}\right)1,500 =$$
$$\left(\frac{6}{5}\right)1,500 =$$
$$(6)300 = 1,800$$

You are solving for y, which represents the percent change of 1,800:

$$\text{Percent Change} = \frac{\text{Change in Value}}{\text{Original Value}}$$

The change in value from 1,800 to 1,080 is 1,800 − 1,080 = 720:

$$\frac{y}{100} = \frac{720}{1,800}$$

You can save time by noticing that 720 and 1,800 are both divisible by 360:

$$\frac{y}{100} = \frac{2}{5}$$

$$y = \frac{200}{5} = 40$$

y is equal to 40%.

Alternatively, you can treat the whole question as one successive percent.

If 1,500 is increased by 20%, then decreased by y%, then 1,080 IS 120% of $(100 - y)$% of 1,500:

$$1,080 = \left(\frac{120}{100}\right)\left(\frac{100 - y}{100}\right)1,500$$
$$1,080 = \left(\frac{6}{5}\right)(100 - y)15$$
$$1,080 = (6)(100 - y)3$$
$$1,080 = 18(100 - y)$$
$$60 = 100 - y$$
$$y = 40$$

10. **480 mL**: You can begin by figuring out what the total amount of liquid is.

If the bottle was 80% full, and adding 200 mL of rum made the bottle full, then 200 mL is equal to 20% of the total capacity of the bottle. Let b be the total capacity of the bottle:

$$200 = \frac{20}{100}b$$
$$200 = \frac{1}{5}b$$
$$1,000 = b$$

The bottle has a total capacity of 1,000 mL.

Now you can use a successive percent to figure out the total amount of guava juice. 80% of the bottle is filled with juice, and 60% of the juice is guava juice. In other words, guava juice is 60% of 80% of 1,000 mL:

$$g = \left(\frac{60}{100}\right)\left(\frac{80}{100}\right)1{,}000$$

$$g = \left(\frac{3}{5}\right)\left(\frac{4}{5}\right)1{,}000$$

$$g = \left(\frac{3}{1}\right)\left(\frac{4}{1}\right)40$$

$$g = 3 \times 160$$

$$g = 480$$

There is 480 mL of guava juice.

Note that the last calculation, $3 \times 4 \times 40$, can be done in any order that is easiest for you. Most of the time, multiplying the largest numbers together first is easier in the long run

Chapter *of* 4

Fractions, Decimals, & Percents

Ratios

In This Chapter...

Label Each Part of the Ratio with Units

Proportions

The Unknown Multiplier

Multiple Ratios: Make a Common Term

Chapter 4:

Ratios

A ratio expresses a particular relationship between two or more quantities. Here are some examples of ratios:

> The two partners spend time working in the ratio of 1 to 3. For every 1 hour the first partner works, the second partner works 3 hours.

> Three sisters invest in a certain stock in the ratio of 2 to 3 to 8. For every $2 the first sister invests, the second sister invests $3, and the third sister invests $8.

> The ratio of men to women in the room is 3 to 4. For every 3 men, there are 4 women.

Ratios can be expressed in different ways:

> 1. Using the word "to," as in 3 to 4
> 2. Using a colon, as in $3:4$
> 3. By writing a fraction, as in $\dfrac{3}{4}$ (only for ratios of 2 quantities)

Ratios can express a part-part relationship or a part-whole relationship:

> A part–part relationship: The ratio of men to women in the office is $3:4$.
> A part–whole relationship: There are 3 men for every 7 employees.

Notice that if there are only two parts in the whole, you can derive a part–whole ratio from a part–part ratio, and vice versa.

The relationship that ratios express is division:

> If the ratio of men to women in the office is $3:4$, then the number of men *divided by* the number of women equals $\dfrac{3}{4}$, or 0.75.

Remember that ratios only express a *relationship* between two or more items; they do not provide enough information, on their own, to determine the exact quantity for each item. For example, knowing that the ratio of men to women in an office is 3 to 4 does NOT tell us exactly how many men and how many women are in the office. All you know is that the number of men is $\frac{3}{4}$ the number of women. However, ratios are surprisingly powerful on Data Sufficiency. They often provide enough information to answer the question.

If two quantities have a **constant ratio**, they are in direct proportion to each other.

If the number of men is directly proportional to the number of women, then the number of men divided by the number of women is some constant.

Label Each Part of the Ratio with Units

The order in which a ratio is given is vital. For example, "the ratio of dogs to cats is $2:3$" is very different from "the ratio of dogs to cats is $3:2$." The first ratio says that for every 2 dogs, there are 3 cats. The second ratio says that for every 3 dogs, there are 2 cats.

It is very easy to accidentally reverse the order of a ratio—especially on a timed test like the GMAT. Therefore, to avoid these reversals, always write units on either the ratio itself or on the variables you create, or on both.

Thus, if the ratio of dogs to cats is $2:3$, you can write $\frac{x \text{ dogs}}{y \text{ cats}} = \frac{2 \text{ dogs}}{3 \text{ cats}}$, or simply $\frac{x \text{ dogs}}{y \text{ cats}} = \frac{2}{3}$, or even

$\frac{D}{C} = \frac{2 \text{ dogs}}{3 \text{ cats}}$, where D and C are variables standing for the number of dogs and cats, respectively.

However, do not just write $\frac{x}{y} = \frac{2}{3}$. You could easily forget which variable stands for cats and which for dogs.

Also, ***never*** write $\frac{2d}{3c}$. The reason is that you might think that d and c stand for *variables*—that is, numbers in their own right. Always write the full unit out.

Proportions

Simple ratio problems can be solved with a proportion:

> The ratio of girls to boys in the class is 4 to 7. If there are 35 boys in the class, how many girls are there?

Step 1: Set up a labeled proportion:

$$\frac{4 \text{ girls}}{7 \text{ boys}} = \frac{x \text{ girls}}{35 \text{ boys}}$$

Step 2: Cross-multiply to solve:

$$140 = 7x$$
$$x = 20$$

To save time, you should cancel factors out of proportions before cross-multiplying. You can cancel factors either vertically within a fraction or horizontally across an equals sign:

$$\frac{4 \text{ girls}}{7 \text{ boys}} = \frac{x \text{ girls}}{35 \text{ boys}} \qquad \frac{4 \text{ girls}}{\cancel{7} \, 1 \text{ boy}} = \frac{x \text{ girls}}{\cancel{35} \, 5 \text{ boys}} \qquad x = 20$$

Never cancel factors diagonally across an equals sign. Always cross-multiply.

The Unknown Multiplier

For more complicated ratio problems, the **Unknown Multiplier** technique is useful. For example:

> The ratio of men to women in a room is $3:4$. If there are 56 people in the room, how many of the people are men?

Using the methods from the previous page, you can write the ratio relationship as $\dfrac{M \text{ men}}{W \text{ women}} = \dfrac{3}{4}$.

Together with $M + W = \text{Total} = 56$, you can solve for M (and W, for that matter). The algebra for these "two equations and two unknowns" is not too difficult.

However, there is even an easier way. It requires a slight shift in your thinking, but if you can make this shift, you can save yourself a lot of work on some problems. Instead of representing the number of men as M, represent it as $3x$, where x is some unknown (positive) number. Likewise, instead of representing the number of women as W, represent it as $4x$, where x is the same unknown number.

What does this seemingly odd step accomplish? It guarantees that the ratio of men to women is $3:4$. The ratio of men to women can now be expressed as $\dfrac{3x}{4x}$, which reduces to $\dfrac{3}{4}$, the desired ratio. (Note that you can cancel the x's because you know that x is not zero.) This variable x is known as the Unknown Multiplier. The Unknown Multiplier allows you to reduce the number of variables, making the algebra easier.

Now determine the value of the Unknown Multiplier using the other equation:

$$\text{Men} + \text{Women} = \text{Total} = 56$$
$$3x + 4x = 56$$
$$7x = 56$$
$$x = 8$$

4

Now you know that the value of x, the Unknown Multiplier, is 8. Therefore, you can determine the exact number of men and women in the room:

The number of men $= 3x = 3(8) = 24$. The number of women $= 4x = 4(8) = 32$.

When *can* you use the Unknown Multiplier? You can use it *once* per problem. Every other ratio in the problem must be set up with a proportion. You should never have two Unknown Multipliers in the same problem.

When *should* you use the Unknown Multiplier? You should use it when neither quantity in the ratio is already equal to a number or a variable expression. Generally, the first ratio in a problem can be set up with an Unknown Multiplier. In the "girls & boys" problem on the previous page, however, you can glance ahead and see that the number of boys is given as 35. This means that you can just set up a simple proportion to solve the problem.

The Unknown Multiplier is particularly useful with three-part ratios. For example:

A recipe calls for amounts of lemon juice, wine, and water in the ratio of 2:5:7. If all three combined yield 35 milliliters of liquid, how much wine was included?

Make a quick table:

Lemon Juice	+	Wine	+	Water	=	Total
$2x$	+	$5x$	+	$7x$	=	$14x$

Now solve: $14x = 35$, or $x = 2.5$. Thus, the amount of wine is $5x = 5(2.5) = 12.5$ milliliters.

In this problem, the Unknown Multiplier turns out not to be an integer. This result is fine, because the problem deals with continuous quantities (milliliters of liquids). In problems like the first one, which deals with integer quantities (men and women), the Unknown Multipier must be a positive integer. In that specific problem, the multiplier is literally the number of "complete sets" of 3 men and 4 women each.

Multiple Ratios: Make a Common Term

You may encounter two ratios containing a common element. To combine the ratios, you can use a process remarkably similar to creating a common denominator for fractions.

Because ratios act like fractions, you can multiply both sides of a ratio (or all sides, if there are more than two) by the same number, just as you can multiply the numerator and denominator of a fraction by the same number. You can change *fractions* to have common *denominators*. Likewise, you can change *ratios* to have common *terms* corresponding to the same quantity. Consider the following problem:

> In a box containing action figures of the three Fates from Greek mythology, there are three figures of Clotho for every two figures of Atropos, and five figures of Clotho for every four figures of Lachesis.
>
> (a)   What is the least number of action figures that could be in the box?
> (b)   What is the ratio of Lachesis figures to Atropos figures?

(a) In symbols, this problem tells you that $C:A = 3:2$ and $C:L = 5:4$. You cannot instantly combine these ratios into a single ratio of all three quantities, because the terms for C are different. However, you can fix that problem by multiplying each ratio by the right number, making both C's into the *least common multiple* of the current values:

$$
\begin{array}{lll}
\underline{C\,:\,A\,:\,L} & & \underline{C\,:\,A\,:\,L} \\
3\,:\,2 & \rightarrow \quad \text{Multiply by 5} \quad \rightarrow & 15:10 \\
5\,:\quad:\,4 & \rightarrow \quad \text{Multiply by 3} \quad \rightarrow & 15:\quad:12 \\
& \text{This is the combined ratio:} & \boxed{15:10:12}
\end{array}
$$

The *actual* numbers of action figures are these three numbers times an Unknown Multiplier, which must be a positive integer. Using the smallest possible multiplier, 1, there are $15 + 12 + 10 = 37$ action figures.

(b) Once you have combined the ratios, you can extract the numbers corresponding to the quantities in question and disregard the others: $L:A = 12:10$, which reduces to $6:5$.

'48
96
/144   3

6.6
:36
6
/196
3% = 56.6
6

2

4.4

Problem Set

Solve the following problems, using the strategies you have learned in this section. Use proportions and the Unknown Multiplier to organize ratios.

For problems 1 through 5, assume that neither x nor y is equal to 0, to permit division by x and by y.

1. $48:2x$ is equivalent to $144:600$. What is x? $x = 100$

2. $2x:y$ is equivalent to $4x:8,500$. What is y? 4250

3.   Brian's marbles have a red to yellow ratio of $2:1$. If Brian has 22 red marbles, how many yellow marbles does Brian have? 11

4.   Initially, the men and women in a room were in the ratio of $5:7$. Six women leave the room. If there are 35 men in the room, how many women are left in the room?
      $x = 49 \quad -6 = 43$ $5:7$
                                                                     $35:7x$

5.   The amount of time that three people worked on a special project was in the ratio of 2 to 3 to 5. If the project took 110 hours, how many more hours did the hardest working person work than the person who worked the least?
                                                                     $2:3:5$
      33 $2x \quad 10x = 110$
                                                                     $x = 11$
6.   Alexandra needs to mix cleaning solution in the following ratio: 1 part bleach for $22 \quad 55$
      every 4 parts water. When mixing the solution, Alexandra makes a mistake and
      mixes in half as much bleach as she ought to have. The total solution consists of 27
      mL. How much bleach did Alexandra put into the solution? $1:4$
      $3 \; parts$ $1:8$
                                                                                $9 \qquad 27$
7.   If the scale model of a cube sculpture is 0.5 cm per every 1 m of the real sculpture, $3 \quad 3:24$
      what is the volume of the model, if the volume of the real sculpture is 64 m³?

                                    $0.5:100$

Solutions

1. **100:**

$$\frac{48}{2x} = \frac{144}{600}$$ Simplify the ratios and cancel factors horizontally across the equals sign.

$$\frac{\cancel{48}\ 24}{\cancel{2x}\ x} = \frac{\cancel{144}\ 12}{\cancel{600}\ 50}$$

$$\frac{\cancel{24}\ 4}{x} = \frac{\cancel{6}\ 1}{25}$$

$$\frac{2}{x} = \frac{1}{50}$$

$$x = 100$$ Then, cross-multiply: $x = 100$.

2. **4,250:**

$$\frac{2x}{y} = \frac{4x}{8,500}$$ First, simplify the ratio on the right-hand side of the equation.

$$\frac{2x}{y} = \frac{x}{2,125}$$ Then, cross-multiply: $4,250x = xy$.
Divide both sides of the equation by x: $y = 4,250$.

3. **11:** Write a proportion to solve this problem: $\dfrac{\text{red}}{\text{yellow}} = \dfrac{2}{1} = \dfrac{22}{x}$.

   Cross-multiply to solve: $2x = 22$
   $$x = 11$$

4. **43:** First, establish the starting number of men and women with a proportion, and simplify:

$$\frac{5 \text{ men}}{7 \text{ women}} = \frac{35 \text{ men}}{x \text{ women}} \qquad \frac{\cancel{5}\ 1 \text{ man}}{7 \text{ women}} = \frac{\cancel{35}\ 7 \text{ men}}{x \text{ women}}$$

   Cross-multiply: $x = 49$.

If 6 women leave the room, there are $49 - 6 = 43$ women left.

5. **33 hours:** Use an equation with the Unknown Multiplier to represent the total hours put in by the three people:

$$2x + 3x + 5x = 110$$
$$10x = 110$$
$$x = 11$$

Therefore, the hardest working person put in $5(11) = 55$ hours, and the person who worked the least put in $2(11) = 22$ hours. This represents a difference of $55 - 22 = 33$ hours.

6. **3 mL:** The correct ratio is $1:4$, which means that there should be x parts bleach and $4x$ parts water. However, Alexandra put in half as much bleach as she should have, so she put in $\dfrac{x}{2}$ parts bleach. You can represent this with an equation: $\dfrac{x}{2} + 4x = 27$.

$$x + 8x = 54$$
$$9x = 54$$
$$x = 6$$

You were asked to find how much bleach Alexandra used. This equalled $x/2$, so Alexandra used $6/2 = 3$ mL of bleach.

7. **8 cm³:**

Real: $V = s^3 \rightarrow 64 = s^3 \rightarrow s = 4$	The length of a side on the real sculpture is 4 m.
$\dfrac{Model}{Real} : \dfrac{0.5 \text{ cm}}{1 \text{ m}} = \dfrac{x \text{ cm}}{4 \text{ m}}$	Set up a proportion and solve for x, the side of the model
$\dfrac{0.5}{1} = \dfrac{x}{4}$	
$x = 2$ cm	The length of a side on the model is 2 cm.
Model: $V = s^3 = (2)^3 = 8$	The volume of the model is 8 cm³.

Chapter *of* 5

Fractions, Decimals, & Percents

FDPs

In This Chapter. . .

Common FDP Equivalents

Converting Among Fractions, Decimals, and Percents

When to Use Which Form

Chapter 5:

FDPs

GMAT problems often do not test fractions, decimals, and percents in isolation. Instead, many problems that test your understanding of non-integer numbers involve some kind of combination of fractions, decimals, and percents.

For this reason, we refer to these problems as FDPs (an abbreviation for fraction–decimal–percent). In order to achieve success with FDP problems on the GMAT, you must understand the connections between fractions, decimals, and percents; you should be able to shift amongst the three comfortably and quickly. In a very real sense, fractions, decimals, and percents are three different ways of expressing the exact same thing: a part–whole relationship:

> A **fraction** expresses a part–whole relationship in terms of a numerator (the part) and a denominator (the whole).

> A **decimal** expresses a part–whole relationship in terms of place value (a tenth, a hundredth, a thousandth, etc.).

> A **percent** expresses the special part–whole relationship between a number (the part) and one hundred (the whole).

Common FDP Equivalents

You should memorize the following common equivalents:

Fraction	Decimal	Percent
$\frac{1}{100}$	0.01	1%
$\frac{1}{50}$	0.02	2%
$\frac{1}{25}$	0.04	4%
$\frac{1}{20}$	0.05	5%
$\frac{1}{10}$	0.10	10%
$\frac{1}{9}$	$0.\overline{1} \approx 0.111$	$\approx 11.1\%$
$\frac{1}{8}$	0.125	12.5%
$\frac{1}{6}$	$0.1\overline{6} \approx 0.167$	$\approx 16.7\%$
$\frac{1}{5}$	0.2	20%
$\frac{1}{4}$	0.25	25%
$\frac{3}{10}$	0.3	30%
$\frac{1}{3}$	$0.\overline{3} \approx 0.333$	$\approx 33.3\%$
$\frac{3}{8}$	0.375	37.5%
$\frac{2}{5}$	0.4	40%
$\frac{1}{2}$	0.5	50%

Fraction	Decimal	Percent
$\frac{3}{5}$	0.6	60%
$\frac{5}{8}$	0.625	62.5%
$\frac{2}{3}$	$0.\overline{6} \approx 0.667$	$\approx 66.7\%$
$\frac{7}{10}$	0.7	70%
$\frac{3}{4}$	0.75	75%
$\frac{4}{5}$	0.8	80%
$\frac{5}{6}$	$0.8\overline{3} \approx 0.833$	$\approx 83.3\%$
$\frac{7}{8}$	0.875	87.5%
$\frac{9}{10}$	0.9	90%
$\frac{1}{1}$	1	100%
$\frac{5}{4}$	1.25	125%
$\frac{4}{3}$	$1.\overline{3} \approx 1.33$	133%
$\frac{3}{2}$	1.5	150%
$\frac{7}{4}$	1.75	175%

Converting Among Fractions, Decimals, and Percents

The following chart reviews the ways to convert from fractions to decimals, from decimals to fractions, from fractions to percents, from percents to fractions, from decimals to percents, and from percents to decimals.

FROM TO →	FRACTION $\frac{3}{8}$	DECIMAL 0.375	PERCENT 37.5%
FRACTION $\frac{3}{8}$		Divide the numerator by the denominator: $3 \div 8 = 0.375$ Use long division if necessary.	Divide the numerator by the denominator and move the decimal two places to the right: $3 \div 8 = 0.375 \rightarrow 37.5\%$
DECIMAL 0.375	Use the place value of the last digit in the decimal as the denominator, and put the decimal's digits in the numerator. Then simplify: $\frac{375}{1,000} = \frac{3}{8}$		Move the decimal point two places to the right: $0.375 \rightarrow 37.5\%$
PERCENT 37.5%	Use the digits of the percent for the numerator and 100 for the denominator. Then simplify: $\frac{37.5}{100} = \frac{3}{8}$	Find the percent's decimal point and move it two places to the left: $37.5\% \rightarrow 0.375$	

When to Use Which Form

Fractions are good for cancelling factors in multiplications. They are also the best way of exactly expressing proportions that do not have clean decimal equivalents, such as 1/7. Switch to fractions if there is a handy fractional equivalent of the decimal or percent and/or you think you can cancel lots of factors. For example:

What is 37.5% of 240?

If you simply convert the percent to a decimal and multiply, you will have to do a fair bit of arithmetic:

$$\begin{array}{r} 0.375 \\ \times\ 240 \\ \hline 0 \\ 15000 \\ 75000 \\ \hline 90.000 \end{array}$$

Alternatively, you can recognize that $0.375 = \frac{3}{8}$.

So we have $(0.375)(240) = \left(\frac{3}{8}\right)(240\ 30) = 3(30) = 90$.

This is much faster!

A dress is marked up $16\frac{2}{3}\%$ to a final price of \$140. What is the original price of the dress?

From the previous page, you know that $16\frac{2}{3}\%$ is equivalent to $\frac{1}{6}$. Thus, adding $\frac{1}{6}$ of a number to itself is the same thing as multiplying by $1+\frac{1}{6}=\frac{7}{6}$:

$$\frac{7}{6}x=140 \qquad x=\left(\frac{6}{7}\right)140=\left(\frac{6}{7}\right)140\,20=120. \text{ The original price is \$120.}$$

Decimals, on the other hand, are good for estimating results or for comparing sizes. The reason is that the basis of comparison is equivalent (there is no denominator). The same holds true for **percents**. The implied denominator is always 100, so you can easily compare percents (of the same whole) to each other.

To convert certain fractions to decimals or percents, multiply top and bottom by the same number:

$$\frac{17}{25}=\frac{17\times4}{25\times4}=\frac{68}{100}=0.68=68\%$$

This process is faster than long division, but it only works when the denominator has only 2's and/or 5's as factors.

In some cases, you might find it easier to compare a bunch of fractions by giving them all a common denominator, rather than by converting them all to decimals or percents. The general rule is this: **Prefer fractions for doing multiplication or division, but prefer decimals and percents for doing addition or subtraction, for estimating numbers, or for comparing numbers.**

Problem Set

1.   Express the following as fractions and simplify: 2.45   0.008

2.   Express the following as fractions and simplify: 420%   8%

3.   Express the following as decimals and simplify: $\dfrac{9}{2}$ $\dfrac{3,000}{10,000}$

4.   Express the following as decimals and simplify: $1\dfrac{27}{4}$ $12\dfrac{8}{3}$

5.   Express the following as percents: $\dfrac{1,000}{10}$ $\dfrac{25}{8}$

6.   Express the following as percents: 80.4   0.0007

7.   Order from least to greatest: $\dfrac{8}{18}$ 0.8   40%

8.   Order from least to greatest: 1.19 $\dfrac{120}{84}$ 131.44%

9.   What number is 62.5% of 192?

10. 200 is 16% of what number?

Solutions

1. To convert a decimal to a fraction, write it over the appropriate power of 10 and simplify:

$$2.45 = 2\frac{45}{100} = 2\frac{9}{20} \text{ (mixed)} = \frac{49}{20} \text{ (improper)}$$

$$0.008 = \frac{8}{1,000} = \frac{1}{125}$$

2. To convert a percent to a fraction, write it over a denominator of 100 and simplify:

$$420\% = \frac{420}{100} = \frac{21}{5} \text{ (improper)} = 4\frac{1}{5} \text{ (mixed)}$$

$$8\% = \frac{8}{100} = \frac{2}{25}$$

3. To convert a fraction to a decimal, divide the numerator by the denominator:

$$\frac{9}{2} = 9 \div 2 = 4.5$$

It often helps to simplify the fraction *before* you divide:

$$\frac{3,000}{10,000} = \frac{3}{10} = 0.3$$

4. To convert a mixed number to a decimal, simplify the mixed number first, if needed:

$$1\frac{27}{4} = 1 + 6\frac{3}{4} = 7.75$$

$$12\frac{8}{3} = 12 + 2\frac{2}{3} = 14\frac{2}{3} = 14.\overline{6}$$

Note: You do not have to know the "repeating bar" notation, but you should know that 2/3 = 0.6666....

5. To convert a fraction to a percent, rewrite the fraction with a denominator of 100:

$$\frac{1,000}{10} = \frac{10,000}{100} = 10,000\%$$

Or, convert the fraction to a decimal and shift the decimal point two places to the right:

$$\frac{25}{8} = 25 \div 8 = 3\frac{1}{8} = 3.125 = 312.5\%$$

6. To convert a decimal to a percent, shift the decimal point two places to the right:

$$80.4 = 8,040\%$$
$$0.0007 = 0.07\%$$

7. $\mathbf{40\% < \dfrac{8}{18} < 0.8}$: To order from least to greatest, express all the terms in the same form:

$$\frac{8}{18} = \frac{4}{9} = 0.4444\ldots = 0.\overline{4}$$

$0.8 = 0.8$
$40\% = 0.4$
$0.4 < 0.\overline{4} < 0.8$

8. $\mathbf{1.19 < 131.44\% < \dfrac{120}{84}}$: To order from least to greatest, express all the terms in the same form:

$1.19 = 1.19$

$$\frac{120}{84} \approx 1.4286$$

$131.44\% = 1.3144$
$1.19 < 1.3144 < 1.4286$

9. **120:** This is a percent vs. decimal conversion problem. If you simply recognize that $62.5\% = 0.625$ $= \dfrac{5}{8}$, this problem will be a lot easier: $\dfrac{5}{8} \times 192 = \dfrac{5}{1} \times 24 = 120$. Multiplying 0.625×240 will take much longer to complete.

10. **1,250:** This is a percent vs. decimal conversion problem. If you simply recognize that $16\% = 0.16 = \dfrac{16}{100} = \dfrac{4}{25}$, this problem will be a lot easier: $\dfrac{4}{25}x = 200$, so $x = 200 \times \dfrac{25}{4} = 50 \times 25 = 1,250$. Dividing out $200 \div 0.16$ will probably take longer to complete.

Chapter 6
of
Fractions, Decimals, & Percents

FDP Strategies

In This Chapter...

Data Sufficiency Basics

What Does "Sufficient" Mean?

The DS Process

Putting It All Together

Putting It All Together (Again)

Concrete Values vs. Relative Values

Smart Numbers: Multiples of the Denominators

When Not to Use Smart Numbers

Smart Numbers: Pick 100

Benchmark Values

Chapter 6:
FDP Strategies

The following five sections appear in all 5 quant strategy guides. If you are familiar with this information, skip ahead to page 92 for new content.

Data Sufficiency Basics

Every Data Sufficiency problem has the *same* basic form:

> The **Question Stem** is (sometimes) made up of two parts:
>
> (1) The **Question**: *"What day of the week is the party on?"*
> (2) Possible **Additional Info**: *"Jon's birthday party is this week."*
>   This might simply be background OR could provide additional constraints or equations needed to solve the problem.

Jon's birthday party is this week. What day of the week is the party on?

    (1)   The party is not on Monday or Tuesday.
    (2)   The party is not on Wednesday, Thursday, or Friday.

(A)   Statement (1) ALONE is sufficient, but statement (2) is NOT sufficient
(B)   Statement (2) ALONE is sufficient, but statement (1) is NOT sufficient
(C)   BOTH statements TOGETHER are sufficient, but NEITHER statement ALONE is sufficient
(D)   EACH statement ALONE is sufficient
(E)   Statements (1) and (2) TOGETHER are NOT sufficient

> Following the question are **two Statements** labeled (1) and (2).
>
> To answer Data Sufficiency problems correctly, you need to decide **whether the statements provide enough information to answer the question**. In other words, do you have *sufficient data*?

> Lastly, you are given the **Answer Choices**.
>
> These are the *same* for every Data Sufficiency problem so **memorize them** as soon as possible.

What Does "Sufficient" Mean?

The key to Data Sufficiency is to remember that it *does not* require you to answer the question asked in the question stem. Instead, you need to decide whether the statements provide enough information to answer the question.

Notice that in answer choices (A), (B), and (D), you are asked to evaluate each of the statements separately. You must then decide if the information given in each is sufficient (on its own) to answer the question in the stem.

The correct answer choice will be:

> **(A)** when Statement (1) provides enough information by itself, but Statement (2) does not,
> **(B)** when Statement (2) provides enough information by itself, but Statement (1) does not,
> OR
> **(D)** when BOTH statements, *independently*, provide enough information.

But what happens when you cannot answer the question with *either* statement individually? Now you must put them together and decide if all of the information given is sufficient to answer the question in the stem.

If you **must** use the statements together, the correct answer choice will be:

> **(C)** if together they provide enough information (but neither alone is sufficient),
> OR
> **(E)** if the statements, even together, do not provide enough information.

We will revisit the answer choices when we discuss a basic process for Data Sufficiency.

The DS Process

Data Sufficiency tests logical reasoning as much as it tests mathematical concepts. In order to master Data Sufficiency, develop a consistent process that will help you stay on task. It is very easy to forget what you are actually trying to accomplish as you answer these questions.

To give yourself the best chance of consistently answering DS questions correctly, you need to be methodical. The following steps can help reduce errors on every DS problem.

Step 1: Separate *additional info* from the *actual question.*

If the additional information contains *constraints* or *equations*, make a note on your scrap paper.

Step 2: Determine whether the question is Value or Yes/No.

Value: The **question** asks for the value of an unknown (e.g., What is x?).

A statement is **Sufficient** when it provides **1 possible value**.
A statement is **Not Sufficient** when it provides **more than 1 possible value**.

Yes/No: The **question** that is asked has two possible answers: Yes or No (e.g., Is x even?).

A statement is **Sufficient** when it provides a **definite Yes or definite No**.
A statement is **Not Sufficient** when the answer **could be Yes or No**.

	Sufficient	Not Sufficient
Value	**1 Value**	**More than 1 Value**
Yes/No	**1 Answer (Yes or No)**	**More than 1 Answer (Yes AND No)**

Step 3: Decide *exactly* what the question is asking.

To properly evaluate the statements, you must have a very precise understanding of the question asked in the question stem. Ask yourself two questions:

1. What, *precisely*, would be *sufficient*?
2. What, *precisely*, would *not* be *sufficient*?

For instance, suppose the question is, "What is x?"

1. What, precisely, would be sufficient? **One value for x** (e.g., $x = 5$).
2. What, precisely, would not be sufficient? **More than one value for x** (e.g., x is prime).

Step 4: Use the Grid to evaluate the statements.

The answer choices need to be evaluated in the proper order. The Grid is a simple but effective tool to help you keep track of your progress. Write the following on your page:

AD
BCE

The two columns below will tell you how to work through the Grid:

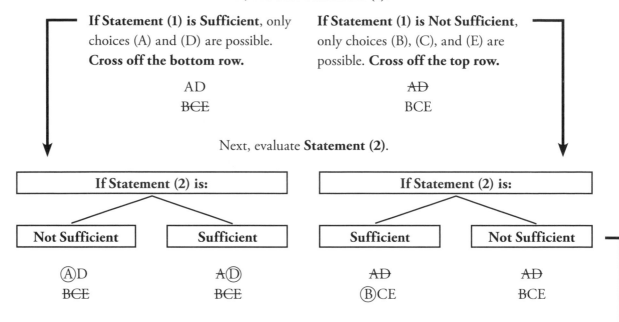

First, **evaluate Statement (1)**.

If Statement (1) is Sufficient, only choices (A) and (D) are possible. **Cross off the bottom row.**

If Statement (1) is Not Sufficient, only choices (B), (C), and (E) are possible. **Cross off the top row.**

AD
~~BCE~~

~~AD~~
BCE

Next, evaluate **Statement (2)**.

If Statement (2) is:

Not Sufficient | Sufficient

Ⓐ D
~~BCE~~

A Ⓓ
~~BCE~~

If Statement (2) is:

Sufficient | Not Sufficient

~~AD~~
Ⓑ CE

~~AD~~
BCE

Notice that the first two steps are always the same: evaluate Statement (1) then evaluate Statement (2).

If neither Statement by itself is sufficient, then the only two possible answers are (C) and (E). The next step is to look at the Statements TOGETHER:

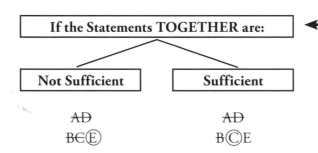

If the Statements TOGETHER are:

Not Sufficient | Sufficient

~~AD~~
~~BC~~Ⓔ

~~AD~~
B Ⓒ E

Putting It All Together

Now that you know the process, it's time to work through the practice problem start to finish.

Jon's birthday party is this week. What day of the week is the party on?

(1) The party is not on Monday or Tuesday.
(2) The party is not on Wednesday, Thursday, or Friday.

(A) Statement (1) ALONE is sufficient, but statement (2) is NOT sufficient
(B) Statement (2) ALONE is sufficient, but statement (1) is NOT sufficient
(C) BOTH statements TOGETHER are sufficient, but NEITHER statement ALONE is sufficient
(D) EACH statement ALONE is sufficient
(E) Statements (1) and (2) TOGETHER are NOT sufficient

handwritten note: AD BCE depending if statement 1 is sufficient

Step 1: Separate *additional info* from the *actual question*.

<u>Question</u>	<u>Additional Info</u>
What day of the week is the party on?	Jon's birthday party is this week.

Step 2: Determine whether the question is Value or Yes/No.

You need to know the exact day of the week that the party is on.

This is a Value question.

Step 3: Decide *exactly* what the question is asking.

What, precisely, would be sufficient? **One possible day of the week.**
What, precisely, would not be sufficient? **More than one possible day of the week.**

Step 4: Use the Grid to evaluate the statements.

Evaluate Statement (1): Statement (1) tells you that the party is *not* on Monday or Tuesday. The party could still be on Wednesday, Thursday, Friday, Saturday, or Sunday. Statement (1) is Not Sufficient.

~~AD~~
BCE

Evaluate Statement (2): Statement (2) tells you that the party is *not* on Wednesday, Thursday, or Friday. The party could still be on Saturday, Sunday, Monday, or Tuesday. Statement (2) is Not Sufficient.

~~AD~~
~~BCE~~

Now that you've verified neither statement is sufficient on its own, it's time to evaluate the statements taken together.

Evaluate (1) AND (2): Taking both statements together, you know the party is not on Monday, Tuesday, Wednesday, Thursday, or Friday. The party could still be on Saturday or Sunday. Statements (1) and (2) together are Not Sufficient.

~~AD~~
~~BC~~(E)

The correct answer is **(E)**.

Putting It All Together (Again)

Now try a different, but related, question:

> It rains all day every Saturday and Sunday in Seattle, and never on any other day. Is it raining in Seattle right now?
>
> (1) Today is not Monday or Tuesday.
> (2) Today is not Wednesday, Thursday, or Friday.

(A) Statement (1) ALONE is sufficient, but statement (2) is NOT sufficient

(B) Statement (2) ALONE is sufficient, but statement (1) is NOT sufficient

(C) BOTH statements TOGETHER are sufficient, but NEITHER statement ALONE is sufficient

(D) EACH statement ALONE is sufficient

(E) Statements (1) and (2) TOGETHER are NOT sufficient

The statements are exactly the same as in the previous example, but the question has changed. The process is still the same.

Step 1: Separate *additional info* from the *actual question*.

Question	Additional Info
Is it raining in Seattle right now?	It rains all day every Saturday and Sunday in Seattle, and never on any other day.

Step 2: Determine whether the question is Value or Yes/No.

There are two possible answers to this question:

1.   Yes, it is raining in Seattle right now.
2.   No, it is not raining in Seattle right now.

This is a Yes/No question.

Step 3: Decide *exactly* what the question is asking.

Be careful. This part of the process is usually more complicated when the question is Yes/No. Sufficient is defined as providing a definite answer to the Yes/No question. Since the statements often allow for multiple possible values, you have to ask the Yes/No question for all the possible values.

Before you look at the statements, keep in mind there are only 7 days of the week. You know the answer to the question on each of those days as well. If today is Saturday or Sunday, the answer is **yes, it is raining in Seattle right now**. If today is Monday, Tuesday, Wednesday, Thursday, or Friday, the answer is **no, it is not raining in Seattle right now**.

What, precisely, would be sufficient? **It is definitely raining (Saturday or Sunday) OR it is definitely NOT raining (Monday through Friday).**
What, precisely, would not be sufficient? **It may be raining (e.g., Today is either Friday or Saturday).**

Step 4: Use the Grid to evaluate the statements.

Evaluate Statement (1): Statement (1) tells you that today is *not* Monday or Tuesday. Today could still be Wednesday, Thursday, Friday, Saturday, or Sunday. It might be raining in Seattle right now. You cannot know for sure. Statement (1) is Not Sufficient.

~~AD~~
BCE

Evaluate Statement (2): Statement (2) tells you that today is *not* Wednesday, Thursday, or Friday. Today could still be Saturday, Sunday, Monday, or Tuesday. It might be raining in Seattle right now. You cannot know for sure. Statement (2) is Not Sufficient.

~~AD~~
~~B~~CE

Now that you've verified neither statement is sufficient on its own, it's time to evaluate the statement taken together.

Evaluate (1) AND (2): Taking both statements together, you know that today is not Monday, Tuesday, Wednesday, Thursday, or Friday. Today could still be on Saturday or Sunday. If today is Saturday, you know that it is raining in Seattle. If today is Sunday, you know that it is raining in Seattle. Either way, you can say definitely that **yes, it is raining in Seattle right now**. Taken together, Statements (1) and (2) are Sufficient.

~~AD~~
~~B~~ⒸE

The correct answer is (C).

Concrete Values vs. Relative Values

The GMAT likes using Fractions, Decimals, Percents, and Ratios (FDPRs) in Data Sufficiency questions because a little information can go a long way.

This section will talk about FDPR word problems. There are two types of information presented in these problems: concrete values and relative values.

    1. **Concrete values** are actual amounts (# of tickets sold, liters of water, etc.), and

    2. **relative values** relate two quantities using fractions, decimals, percents, or ratios (twice as many, 60% less, ratio of $2:3$, etc.).

A company sells only two kinds of pie: apple pie and cherry pie. What fraction of the total pies sold last month were apple pies?	A company sells only two kinds of pie: apple pie and cherry pie. How many apple pies did the company sell last month?
(1) The company sold 460 pies last month.	(1) The company sold 460 pies last month.
(2) The company sold 30% more cherry pies than apple pies last month.	(2) The company sold 30% more cherry pies than apple pies last month.

The question itself will also ask for either a concrete value or a relative value.

The question on the right asks for a concrete value (How many apple pies) while the question on the left asks for a relative value (What fraction of the pies).

The difference is important because you need *more* information to find a concrete value.

Take a look at the question on the left first. You can label the number of apple pies sold a and the number of cherry pies sold c.

You need to know what fraction of the total pies sold were apple pies:

$$\frac{\text{apple pies}}{\text{total pies}} = ?$$

The total number of apple pies sold is a, and the total number of pies sold is $a + c$.

$$\frac{a}{a+c} = ?$$

Look at Statement 1. If the total number of pies sold was 460, then $a + c = 460$. You can plug this value into your question:

MANHATTAN
GMAT

$$\frac{a}{460} = ?$$

You don't have enough information to answer the question. Eliminate answer choices (A) and (D).

Now look at Statement 2. If the company sold 30% more cherry pies than apple pies, then the number of cherry pies sold was 130% of the number of apple pies sold:

$$1.3a = c$$

On the surface this may not seem like enough information. But watch what happens if you replace c with $1.3a$ in the rephrased question.

$$\frac{a}{a+c} = ?$$
$$\frac{a}{a+1.3a} =$$
$$\frac{a}{2.3a} = \frac{1}{2.3}$$

Statement 2 gave you enough information to find the value of our fraction. The correct answer is (B).

Now the question becomes, is there a way you could have recognized sooner that Statement 2 was sufficient? Yes, there is!

Remember that this Data Sufficiency question was asking for a relative value (What fraction of the pies). Relative values are intimately related to ratios. The ratio in this question is:

apple pies sold : cherry pies sold : total pies sold.

One way to rephrase the question is to say that it asked for the ratio of apple pies sold to total pies sold. Statement 2 was sufficient because it provides the ratio of apple pies sold to cherry pies sold.

If a Data Sufficiency question asks for the relative value of two pieces of a ratio, ANY statement that gives the relative value of ANY two pieces of the ratio will be sufficient.

Try contrasting this to the question that asked for a concrete value:

A company sells only two kinds of pie: apple pie and cherry pie. How many apple pies did the company sell last month?

(1) The company sold 460 pies last month.
(2) The company sold 30% more cherry pies than apple pies last month.

This question is asking for the value of a.

Take a look at Statement 1:

$a + c = 460$

Without the value of c, this will not allow you to solve for a. You can eliminate answer choices (A) and (D).

Now look at Statement 2:

$1.3a = c$

Once again, without the value of c, you can't solve for the value of a. Cross off answer choice (B).

Now look at the two statements together:

$a + c = 460$
$1.3a = c$

With two variables and two equations, you'll be able to solve for the value of a. Together, the statements are sufficient. The right answer is **(C)**.

Once again, there is a general principle here. Statement 1 provided a concrete value for the total number of pies sold. Statement 2 provided the ratio of apple pies sold to cherry pies sold (a relative value).

If a Data Sufficiency question asks for the concrete value of one element of a ratio, you will need BOTH the concrete value of another element of the ratio AND the relative value of two elements of the ratio.

Smart Numbers: Multiples of the Denominators

Sometimes, fraction problems on the GMAT include unspecified numerical amounts; often these unspecified amounts are described by variables. In these cases, pick real numbers to stand in for the variables. To make the computation easier, choose **Smart Numbers** equal to common multiples of the denominators of the fractions in the problem.

For example, consider this problem:

> The Crandalls' hot tub is half filled. Their swimming pool, which has a capacity four times that of the tub, is filled to four-fifths of its capacity. If the hot tub is drained into the swimming pool, to what fraction of its capacity will the pool be filled?

The denominators in this problem are 2 and 5. The Smart Number is the least common denominator, which is 10. Therefore, assign the hot tub a capacity of 10 units. Since the swimming pool has a capacity 4 times that of the pool, the swimming pool has a capacity of 40 units. You know that the hot tub is only half filled; therefore, it has 5 units of water in it. The swimming pool is four-fifths of the way filled, so it has 32 units of water in it.

Add the 5 units of water from the hot tub to the 32 units of water that are already in the swimming pool: $32 + 5 = 37$.

With 37 units of water and a total capacity of 40, the pool will be filled to $\dfrac{37}{40}$ of its total capacity.

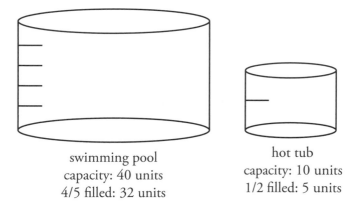

swimming pool
capacity: 40 units
4/5 filled: 32 units

hot tub
capacity: 10 units
1/2 filled: 5 units

When Not to Use Smart Numbers

In some problems, even though an amount might be unknown to you, it is actually specified in the problem in another way. In these cases, you cannot use Smart Numbers to assign real numbers to the variables. For example, consider this problem:

> Mark's comic book collection contains 1/3 Killer Fish comics and 3/8 Shazaam Woman comics. The remainder of his collection consists of Boom! comics. If Mark has 70 Boom! comics, how many comics does he have in his entire collection?

Even though you do not know the number of comics in Mark's collection, you can see that the total is not completely unspecified. You know a piece of the total: 70 Boom! comics. You can use this information to find the total. Do not use Smart Numbers here. Instead, solve similar problems by figuring out how big the known piece is; then, use that knowledge to find the size of the whole. You will need to set up an equation and solve:

$$\dfrac{1}{3} \text{ Killer Fish} + \dfrac{3}{8} \text{ Shazaam Woman} = \dfrac{17}{24} \text{ comics that are } \textit{not} \text{ Boom!}$$

Therefore, $\dfrac{7}{24}$ of the comics are Boom! comics:

$$\frac{7}{24}x = 70$$

$$x = 70 \times \frac{24}{7}$$

$$x = 240$$

Mark has 240 comics.

In summary, **do** pick smart numbers when no amounts are given in the problem, but **do *not*** pick smart numbers when *any* amount or total is given!

Smart Numbers: Pick 100

More often than not, percent problems on the GMAT include unspecified numerical amounts; often these unspecified amounts are described by variables. For example:

> A shirt that initially cost *d* dollars was on sale for 20% off. If *s* represents the sale price of the shirt, *d* is what percentage of *s*?

This is an easy problem that might look confusing. To solve percent problems such as this one, simply pick 100 for the unspecified amount (just as you did when solving successive percents).

If the shirt initially cost $100, then *d* = 100. If the shirt was on sale for 20% off, then the new price of the shirt is $80. Thus, *s* = 80.

The question asks: *d* is what percentage of *s*, or 100 is what percentage of 80? Using a percent table, fill in 80 as the whole and 100 as the part (even though the part happens to be larger than the whole in this case). You are looking for the percent, so set up a proportion, cross-multiply, and solve:

PART	100	x
WHOLE	80	100

$$\frac{100}{80} = \frac{x}{100}$$

$$80x = 10,000 \quad x = 125$$

Therefore, *d* is 125% of *s*.

The important point here is that, like successive percent problems and other percent problems that include unspecified amounts, this example is most easily solved by plugging in a real value. For percent problems, the easiest value to plug in is generally 100. **The fastest way to success with GMAT percent problems with unspecified amounts is to pick 100.**

Benchmark Values

You will use a variety of estimating strategies on the GMAT. One important strategy for estimating with fractions is to use Benchmark Values. These are simple fractions with which you are already familiar:

$$\frac{1}{10}, \frac{1}{5}, \frac{1}{4}, \frac{1}{3}, \frac{1}{2}, \frac{2}{3}, \text{ and } \frac{3}{4}$$

You can use Benchmark Values to compare fractions:

Which is greater: $\frac{127}{255}$ or $\frac{162}{320}$?

If you recognize that 127 is less than half of 255, and 162 is more than half of 320, you will save yourself a lot of cumbersome computation.

You can also use Benchmark Values to estimate computations involving fractions:

What is $\frac{10}{22}$ of $\frac{5}{18}$ of 2,000?

If you recognize that these fractions are very close to the Benchmark Values $\frac{1}{2}$ and $\frac{1}{4}$, you can estimate:

$\frac{1}{2}$ of $\frac{1}{4}$ of 2,000 = 250. Therefore, $\frac{10}{22}$ of $\frac{5}{18}$ of 2,000 ≈ 250.

Notice that the rounding errors compensated for each other:

$\frac{10}{22} \approx \frac{10}{20} = \frac{1}{2}$ You decreased the denominator, so you rounded up: $\frac{10}{22} < \frac{1}{2}$.

$\frac{5}{18} \approx \frac{5}{20} = \frac{1}{4}$ You increased the denominator, so you rounded down: $\frac{5}{18} > \frac{1}{4}$.

If you had rounded $\frac{5}{18}$ to $\frac{6}{18} = \frac{1}{3}$ instead, then you would have rounded **both** fractions up. This would lead to a slight but systematic overestimation:

$$\frac{1}{2} \times \frac{1}{3} \times 2,000 \approx 333$$

Try to make your rounding errors cancel by rounding some numbers up and others down.

6

Benchmark Values: 10%

To find 10% of any number, just move the decimal point to the left one place:

10% of 500 is 50   10% of 34.99 = 3.499   10% of 0.978 is 0.0978

You can use the Benchmark Value of 10% to estimate percents. For example:

> Karen bought a new television, originally priced at $690. However, she had a cou-pon that saved her $67. For what percent discount was Karen's coupon?

You know that 10% of 690 would be 69. Therefore, 67 is slightly less than 10% of 690.

The Heavy Division Shortcut

Some division problems involving decimals can look rather complex. But sometimes, you only need to find an approximate solution. In these cases, you often can save yourself time by using the Heavy Division Shortcut: Move the decimals in the same direction and round to whole numbers. For example:

> What is $1{,}530{,}794 \div (31.49 \times 10^4)$ to the nearest whole number?

Step 1: Set up the division problem in fraction form: $\qquad \dfrac{1{,}530{,}794}{31.49 \times 10^4}$

Step 2: Rewrite the problem, eliminating powers of 10: $\qquad \dfrac{1{,}530{,}794}{314{,}900}$

Step 3: Your goal is to get a single digit to the left of the decimal in the denominator. In this problem, you need to move the decimal point backward 5 spaces. You can do this to the denominator as long as you do the same thing to the numerator. (Technically, what you are doing is dividing top and bottom by the same power of 10: 100,000.) Thus:

$$\frac{1{,}530{,}794}{314{,}900} = \frac{15.30794}{3.14900}$$

Now you have the single digit 3 to the left of the decimal in the denominator.

Step 4: Focus only on the whole number parts of the numerator and denominator and solve: $\qquad \dfrac{15.30794}{3.14900} \approx \dfrac{15}{3} = 5$

An approximate answer to this complex division problem is 5. If this answer is not precise enough, keep one more decimal place and do long division (e.g., $153 \div 31 \approx 4.9$).

MANHATTAN
GMAT

Problem Set

1. Put these fractions in order from least to greatest: $\dfrac{2}{3}$ $\dfrac{3}{13}$ $\dfrac{5}{7}$ $\dfrac{2}{9}$

2. Estimate to the nearest 10,000: $\dfrac{4{,}549{,}982{,}344}{5.342 \times 10^4}$

3. Lisa spends $\dfrac{3}{8}$ of her monthly paycheck on rent and $\dfrac{5}{12}$ on food. Her roommate, Carrie, who earns twice as much as Lisa, spends $\dfrac{1}{4}$ of her monthly paycheck on rent and $\dfrac{1}{2}$ on food. If the two women decide to donate the remainder of their money to charity each month, what fraction of their combined monthly income will they donate?

4. Estimate to the closest integer: What is $\dfrac{11}{30}$ of $\dfrac{6}{20}$ of 120?

5. Rob spends $\dfrac{1}{2}$ of his monthly paycheck, after taxes, on rent. He spends $\dfrac{1}{3}$ on food and $\dfrac{1}{8}$ on entertainment. If he donates the entire remainder, $500, to charity, what is Rob's monthly income, after taxes?

6. Bradley owns b video game cartridges. If Bradley's total is one-third the total owned by Andrew and four times the total owned by Charlie, how many video game cartridges do the three of them own altogether, in terms of b?

   (A) $\dfrac{16}{3}b$ (B) $\dfrac{17}{4}b$ (C) $\dfrac{13}{4}b$ (D) $\dfrac{19}{12}b$ (E) $\dfrac{7}{12}b$

7. Company X has exactly two product lines and no other sources of revenue. If the consumer products line experiences a $k\%$ increase in revenue (where k is a positive integer) in 2010 from 2009 levels and the machine parts line experiences a $k\%$ decrease in revenue in 2010 from 2009 levels, did Company X's overall revenue increase or decrease in 2010?

   (1) In 2009, the consumer products line generated more revenue than the machine parts line.
   (2) $k = 8$

8. Company Z only sells chairs and tables. What percent of its revenue in 2008 did Company Z derive from its sales of chairs?

   (1) In 2008, the price of tables sold by Company Z was 10% higher than the price of chairs sold by Company Z.
   (2) In 2008, Company Z sold 20% fewer tables than chairs.

9. What is the ratio $x : y : z$?

   (1) $x + y = 2z$
   (2) $2x + 3y = z$

P

MANHATTAN
GMAT

Solutions

1. $\dfrac{2}{9} < \dfrac{3}{13} < \dfrac{2}{3} < \dfrac{5}{7}$: Using Benchmark Values, you should notice that $\dfrac{3}{13}$ and $\dfrac{2}{9}$ are both less than $\dfrac{1}{2}$,

and that $\dfrac{2}{3}$ and $\dfrac{5}{7}$ are both more than $\dfrac{1}{2}$. Use cross-multiplication to compare each pair of fractions:

$3 \times 9 = 27$ $\qquad \dfrac{3}{13} \diagup\!\!\!\!\!\diagdown \dfrac{2}{9} \qquad$ $2 \times 13 = 26$ $\qquad\qquad \dfrac{3}{13} > \dfrac{2}{9}$

$2 \times 7 = 14$ $\qquad \dfrac{2}{3} \diagup\!\!\!\!\!\diagdown \dfrac{5}{7} \qquad$ $5 \times 3 = 15$ $\qquad\qquad \dfrac{2}{3} < \dfrac{5}{7}$

This makes it easy to order the fractions: $\dfrac{2}{9} < \dfrac{3}{13} < \dfrac{2}{3} < \dfrac{5}{7}$.

2. **90,000:** Use the Heavy Division Shortcut to estimate:

$$\frac{4{,}549{,}982{,}344}{53{,}420} \approx \frac{4{,}500{,}000{,}000}{50{,}000} = \frac{450{,}000}{5} = 90{,}000$$

3. $\dfrac{17}{72}$: Use Smart Numbers to solve this problem. Since the denominators in the problem are 8, 12,

4, and 2, assign Lisa a monthly paycheck of $24. Assign her roommate, who earns twice as much, a monthly paycheck of $48. The two women's monthly expenses break down as follows:

	Rent	Food	Left over
Lisa	$\dfrac{3}{8}$ of 24 = 9	$\dfrac{5}{12}$ of 24 = 10	24 − (9 + 10) = 5
Carrie	$\dfrac{1}{4}$ of 48 = 12	$\dfrac{1}{2}$ of 48 = 24	48 − (12 + 24) = 12

The women will donate a total of $17 out of their combined monthly income of $72.

4. **Approximately 13:** Use Benchmark Values to estimate: $\dfrac{11}{30}$ is slightly more than $\dfrac{1}{3}$ and $\dfrac{6}{20}$ is

slightly less than $\dfrac{1}{3}$. Therefore, $\dfrac{11}{30}$ of $\dfrac{6}{20}$ of 120 should be approximately $\dfrac{1}{3}$ of $\dfrac{1}{3}$ of 120, or $\dfrac{120}{9}$,

which is slightly more than 13.

Another technique to solve this problem would be to write the product and cancel common factors:

$$\frac{11}{30} \times \frac{6}{20} \times 120 = \frac{(11)(6)(120)}{(30)(20)} = \frac{(11)(120\ 6)}{(5)(20)} = \frac{66}{5} = 13.2$$

Note that for estimation problems, there is not necessarily one best way to estimate. The key is to arrive at an estimate that is close to the exact answer—and to do so quickly!

5. **$12,000:** You cannot use Smart Numbers in this problem, because the total amount is specified. Even though the exact figure is not given in the problem, a portion of the total is specified. This means that the total is a certain number, although you do not know what it is. In fact, the total is exactly what you are being asked to find. Clearly, if you assign a number to represent the total, you will not be able to accurately find the total.

First, use addition to find the fraction of Rob's money that he spends on rent, food, and entertainment: $\frac{1}{2} + \frac{1}{3} + \frac{1}{8} = \frac{12}{24} + \frac{8}{24} + \frac{3}{24} = \frac{23}{24}$. Therefore, the $500 that he donates to charity represents $\frac{1}{24}$ of his total monthly paycheck. We can set up a proportion: $\frac{500}{x} = \frac{1}{24}$. Thus, Rob's monthly income is 500×24, or $12,000.

6. **(B):** This problem can be answered very effectively by picking numbers to represent how many video game cartridges everyone owns. Bradley owns 4 times as many cartridges as Charlie, so you should pick a value for b that is a multiple of 4.

If $b = 4$, then Charlie owns 1 cartridge and Andrew owns 12 cartridges. Together they own $4 + 1 + 12 = 17$ cartridges. Plug $b = 4$ into the answer choices and look for the one that yields 17:

(A) $\frac{16}{3}(4) = \frac{64}{3} = 21\frac{1}{3}$

(B) $\frac{17}{4}(4) = 17$

(C) $\frac{13}{4}(4) = 13$

(D) $\frac{19}{12}(4) = \frac{19}{3} = $ too small to be 17

(E) $\frac{7}{12}(4) = \frac{7}{3} = $ too small to be 17

The correct answer is (B).

7. **(A):** This question requires you to employ logic about percents. No calculation is required, or even possible.

Here's what you know so far (use new variables c and m to keep track of your information):

2009:

consumer products makes c dollars
machine parts makes m dollars
total revenue $= c + m$

2010:

> consumer products makes "*c* dollars increased by *k*%"
> machine parts makes "*m* dollars decreased by *k*%"
> total revenue: ?

What would you need to answer the question, "Did Company X's overall revenue increase or decrease in 2010?" Certainly, if you knew the values of *c*, *m*, and *k*, you could achieve sufficiency, but the GMAT would never write such an easy problem. What is the *minimum* you would need to know to answer definitively?

Since you already know that *k* is a positive integer, you know that *c* increases **by the same percent** by which *m* decreases. So, you don't actually need to know *k*. You already know that *k* percent of whichever number is bigger (*c* or *m*) will constitute a bigger change to the overall revenue.

All this question is asking is whether the overall revenue went up or down. If *c* started off bigger, then a *k*% increase in *c* means more new dollars coming in than you would lose due to a *k*% decrease in the smaller number, *m*. If *c* is smaller, then the *k*% increase would be smaller than what you would lose due to a *k*% decrease in the larger number, *m*.

The question can be rephrased, "Which is bigger, *c* or *m*?"

(1) SUFFICIENT: This statement tells you that *c* is bigger than *m*. Thus, a *k*% increase in *c* is larger than a *k*% decrease in *m*, and the overall revenue went up.

(2) INSUFFICIENT: Knowing the percent change doesn't help, since you don't know whether *c* or *m* is bigger.

Note that you could plug in real numbers if you wanted to, although the problem is faster with logic. Using Statement (1) only:

2009:

> consumer products makes $200
> machine parts makes $100
> total revenue = $300

2010: *if k = 50*

> consumer products makes $300
> machine parts makes $50
> total revenue = $350

You can change *k* to any positive integer (you don't need to know what *k* is). As long as *c* > *m*, you will get the same result. The increase to the larger *c* will be larger than the decrease to the smaller *m*.

The correct answer is (A).

8. **(C):** First of all, notice that the question is only asking for the *percent* of the revenue the company derived from chairs. The question is asking for a relative value.

The revenue for the company can be expressed by the following equation:

$$\text{Revenue}_{\text{Company Z}} = \text{Revenue}_{\text{Tables}} + \text{Revenue}_{\text{Chairs}}$$

If you can find the relative value of *any* two of these Revenues, you will have enough information to answer the question.

Also, note that the GMAT will expect you to know that Revenue = Price × Quantity Sold. This relationship is discussed in more detail in Chapter 1 of the *Word Problems* Strategy Guide.

The revenue derived from tables is the price per table multiplied by the number of tables sold. The revenue derived from chairs is the price per chair multiplied by the number of chairs sold. You can create some variables to represent these unknown values:

$$\text{Revenue}_{\text{Tables}} = P_T \times Q_T$$
$$\text{Revenue}_{\text{Chairs}} = P_C \times Q_C$$

(1) INSUFFICIENT: This statement gives you the relative value of the price of tables to the price of chairs. If the price of tables was 10% higher than the price of chairs, then the price of tables was 110% of the price of chairs:

$$P_T = 1.1P_C$$

However, this information by itself does not give you the relative value of their revenues.

(2) INSUFFICIENT: If the company sold 20% fewer tables than chairs, then the number of tables sold is 80% of the number of chairs sold:

$$Q_T = 0.8Q_C$$

This information by itself, however, does not give you the relative value of their revenues.

(1) AND (2) SUFFICIENT: Look again at the equation for Revenue derived from the sale of tables:

$$\text{Revenue}_{\text{Tables}} = P_T \times Q_T$$

Replace P_T with $1.1P_C$ and replace Q_T with $0.8Q_C$:

$$P_T \times Q_T = (1.1P_C) \times (0.8Q_C)$$
$$P_T \times Q_T = (0.88)(P_C \times Q_C)$$
$$\text{Revenue}_{\text{Tables}} = (0.88)\text{Revenue}_{\text{Chairs}}$$

MANHATTAN
GMAT

Taken together, the two statements provide the relative value of the revenues. No further calculation is required to know that you *can* find the percent of revenue generated from the sale of chairs. The statements together are sufficient.

If you do want to perform the calculation, it would look something like this:

$$\frac{\text{Revenue}_{\text{Chairs}}}{\text{Total Revenue}} = \frac{\text{Revenue}_{\text{Chairs}}}{\text{Revenue}_{\text{Tables}} + \text{Revenue}_{\text{Chairs}}} = \frac{\text{Revenue}_{\text{Chairs}}}{(0.88)\text{Revenue}_{\text{Chairs}} + \text{Revenue}_{\text{Chairs}}} =$$

$$\frac{\text{Revenue}_{\text{Chairs}}}{(1.88)\,\text{Revenue}_{\text{Chairs}}} = \frac{1}{1.88} \approx 53\%$$

Save time on Data Sufficiency questions by avoiding unnecessary computation. Once you know you can find the percent, you should stop and move on to the next problem.

The correct answer is (C).

9. **(C):** For this problem, you do not necessarily need to know the value of x, y, or z. You simply need to know the ratio $x : y : z$ (in other words, the value of x/y AND the value of y/z). You need to manipulate the information given to see whether you can determine this ratio.

(1) INSUFFICIENT: There is no way to manipulate this equation to solve for a ratio. If you simply solve for x/y, for example, you get a variable expression on the other side of the equation:

$$x + y = 2z$$

$$x = 2z - y$$

$$\frac{x}{y} = \frac{2z - y}{y} = \frac{2z}{y} - 1$$

(2) INSUFFICIENT: As in the previous example, there is no way to manipulate this equation to solve for a ratio. If you simply solve for x/y, for example, you get a variable expression on the other side of the equation:

$$2x + 3y = z$$

$$2x = z - 3y$$

$$\frac{x}{y} = \frac{z - 3y}{2y} = \frac{z}{2y} - \frac{3}{2}$$

(1) AND (2) SUFFICIENT: Here, you can use substitution to combine the equations in helpful ways:

$$x + y = 2z$$

$$2x + 3y = z$$

Since $z = 2x + 3y$, you can substitute:

$$x + y = 2(2x + 3y)$$

$$x + y = 4x + 6y$$

Therefore, you can arrive at a value for the ratio x/y:

$$-3x = 5y$$

$$\frac{-3x}{y} = \frac{5\cancel{y}}{\cancel{y}} \qquad \text{Divide by } y.$$

$$\frac{\cancel{-3}x}{\cancel{-3}y} = \frac{5}{-3} \qquad \text{Divide by } -3.$$

$$\frac{x}{y} = \frac{5}{-3}$$

You can also substitute for x to get a value for the ratio y/z:

$$x + y = 2z$$

$$x = 2z - y$$

$$2x + 3y = z$$

$$2(2z - y) + 3y = z$$

$$4z - 2y + 3y = z$$

$$y = -3z$$

$$\frac{y}{z} = -3$$

This tells you that $x : y = -5/3$, and $y/z = -3/1$. Both ratios contain a 3 for the y variable and both also contain a negative sign, so assign the value -3 to y. This means that x must be 5 and z must be 1. Therefore, the ratio $x : y : z = 5 : -3 : 1$.

You can test the result by choosing $x = 5$, $y = -3$, and $z = 1$, or $x = 10$, $y = -6$, and $z = 2$. In either case, the original equations hold up.

The correct answer is (C).

Chapter 7
of
Fractions, Decimals, & Percents

Extra FDPs

In This Chapter...

Repeating Decimals

Terminating Decimals

Using Place Value on the GMAT

The Last Digit Shortcut

Unknown Digits Problems

Formulas That Act on Decimals

Chemical Mixtures

Percents and Weighted Averages

Percent Change and Weighted Averages

Estimating Decimal Equivalents

Chapter 7:

Extra FDPs

This chapter outlines miscellaneous extra topics within the area of *Fractions, Decimals, Percents, & Ratios*.

Repeating Decimals

Dividing an integer by another integer yields a decimal that either terminates or that never ends and repeats itself:

$$2 \div 9 = ?$$

$$
\begin{array}{r}
0.222\ldots \\
9\overline{)2.000} \\
\underline{1.8} \\
20 \\
\underline{18} \\
20
\end{array}
$$

$$2 \div 9 = 0.2222\ldots = 0.\overline{2}$$

The bar above the 2 indicates that the digit 2 repeats forever. You will *not* have to use the bar on the GMAT; it is simply a convenient shorthand.

Generally, you should just do long division to determine the repeating cycle. However, it is worth noting the following patterns, which have appeared in published GMAT questions:

$$4 \div 9 = 0.4444\ldots = 0.\overline{4} \qquad\qquad 23 \div 99 = 0.2323\ldots = 0.\overline{23}$$

$$\frac{1}{11} = \frac{9}{99} = 0.0909\ldots = 0.\overline{09} \qquad\qquad \frac{3}{11} = \frac{27}{99} = 0.2727\ldots = 0.\overline{27}$$

If the denominator is 9, 99, 999 or another number equal to a power of 10 minus 1, then the numerator gives you the repeating digits (perhaps with leading zeroes). Again, you can always find the decimal pattern by simple long division.

Terminating Decimals

Some numbers, like $\sqrt{2}$ and π, have decimals that never end and *never* repeat themselves. The GMAT will only ask you for approximations for these decimals (e.g., $\sqrt{2} \approx 1.4$). Occasionally, though, the GMAT asks you about properties of "terminating" decimals; that is, decimals that end. You can tack on zeroes, of course, but they do not matter. Some examples of terminating decimals are 0.2, 0.47, and 0.375.

Terminating decimals can all be written as a ratio of integers (which might be reducible):

$$\frac{\text{Some integer}}{\text{Some power of 10}}$$

$$0.2 = \frac{2}{10} = \frac{1}{5} \qquad 0.47 = \frac{47}{100} \qquad 0.375 = \frac{375}{1{,}000} = \frac{3}{8}$$

Positive powers of 10 are composed of only 2's and 5's as prime factors. This means that when you reduce this fraction, you only have prime factors of 2's and/or 5's in the denominator. Every terminating decimal shares this characteristic. If, after being fully reduced, the denominator has any prime factors besides 2 or 5, then its decimal will not terminate. If the denominator only has factors of 2 and/or 5, then the decimal will terminate.

Using Place Value on the GMAT

7

Some difficult GMAT problems require the use of place value with unknown digits. For example"

> *A* and *B* are both two-digit numbers, with *A* > *B*. If *A* and *B* contain the same digits, but in reverse order, what integer must be a factor of (*A* − *B*)?
>
> (A) 4　　　　(B) 5　　　　(C) 6　　　　(D) 8　　　　(E) 9

To solve this problem, assign two variables to be the digits in *A* and *B*: *x* and *y*. Let $A = \boxed{x}\boxed{y}$ (***not*** the product of *x* and *y*: *x* is in the tens place, and *y* is in the units place). The boxes remind you that *x* and *y* stand for digits. *A* is therefore the sum of *x* tens and *y* ones. Using algebra, write $A = 10x + y$.

Since *B*'s digits are reversed, $B = \boxed{y}\boxed{x}$. Algebraically, *B* can be expressed as $10y + x$. The difference of *A* and *B* can be expressed as follows:

$$A - B = 10x + y - (10y + x) = 9x - 9y = 9(x - y)$$

Clearly, 9 must be a factor of $A - B$. The correct answer is **(E)**.

You can also make up digits for *x* and *y* and plug them in to create *A* and *B*. This will not necessarily yield the unique right answer, but it should help you eliminate wrong choices.

In general, for unknown digits problems, be ready to create variables (such as x, y, and z) to represent the unknown digits. Recognize that each unknown is restricted to at most 10 possible values (0 through 9). Then apply any given constraints, which may involve number properties such as divisibility or odds & evens.

The Last Digit Shortcut

Sometimes the GMAT asks you to find a units digit, or a remainder after division by 10:

>   What is the units digit of $(7)^2(9)^2(3)^3$?

In this problem, you can use the Last Digit Shortcut:

>   To find the units digit of a product or a sum of integers, only pay attention to the units digits of the numbers you are working with. Drop any other digits.

This shortcut works because only units digits contribute to the units digit of the product:

STEP 1: $7 \times 7 = 49$ Drop the tens digit and keep only the last digit: 9.
STEP 2: $9 \times 9 = 81$ Drop the tens digit and keep only the last digit: 1.
STEP 3: $3 \times 3 \times 3 = 27$ Drop the tens digit and keep only the last digit: 7.
STEP 4: $9 \times 1 \times 7 = 63$ Multiply the last digits of each of the products.

>   The units digit of the final product is 3.

Unknown Digits Problems

Occasionally, the GMAT asks tough problems involving unknown digits. These problems look like "brainteasers"; it seems it could take all day to test the possible digits.

However, like all other GMAT problems, these digit "brainteasers" must be solvable under time constraints. As a result, you always have ways of reducing the number of possibilities:

>   Principles:
>   (1) Look at the answer choices first, to limit your search.
>   (2) Use other given constraints to rule out additional possibilities.
>   (3) Focus on the units digit in the product or sum. This units digit is affected by the fewest other digits.
>   (4) Test the remaining answer choices.

Example:

$$\begin{array}{r} AB \\ \times\ CA \\ \hline DEBC \end{array}$$

In the multiplication above, each letter stands for a different non-zero digit, with $A \times B < 10$. What is the two-digit number AB?

(A) 23   (B) 24   (C) 25   (D) 32   (E) 42

It is often helpful to look at the answer choices. Here, you see that the possible digits for A and B are 2, 3, 4, and 5.

Next, apply the given constraint that $A \times B < 10$. This rules out answer choice (C), 25, since $2 \times 5 = 10$.

Now, test the remaining answer choices. Notice that $A \times B = C$, the units digit of the product. Therefore, you can find all the needed digits and complete each multiplication.

Compare each result to the template. The two positions of the B digit must match:

$$\begin{array}{r} 23 \\ \times\ 62 \\ \hline 1{,}426 \end{array} \qquad\qquad\qquad \begin{array}{r} 24 \\ \times\ 82 \\ \hline 1{,}968 \end{array}$$

The B's do not match   The B's do not match

$$\begin{array}{r} 32 \\ \times\ 63 \\ \hline 2{,}016 \end{array} \qquad\qquad\qquad \begin{array}{r} 42 \\ \times\ 84 \\ \hline 3{,}528 \end{array}$$

The B's do not match   The B's match

Answer is **(E)**.

Note that you could have used the constraints to derive the possible digits (2, 3, and 4) without using the answer choices. However, for these problems, you should take advantage of the answer choices to restrict your search quickly.

Formulas That Act on Decimals

Occasionally, you might encounter a formula or special symbol that acts on decimals. Follow the formula's instructions *precisely*.

Let us define symbol [x] to represent the largest integer less than or equal to x:

What is [5.1]?

According to the definition you are given, [5.1] is the largest integer less than or equal to 5.1. That integer is 5. So [5.1] = 5.

What is [0.8]?

According to the definition again, [0.8] is the largest integer less than or equal to 0.8. That integer is 0. So [0.8] = 0. Notice that the result is **not** 1. This particular definition does not round the number. Rather, the operation *seems* to be truncation—simply cutting off the decimal. However, you must be careful with negatives.

What is [−2.3]?

Once again, [−2.3] is the largest integer less than or equal to −2.3. Remember that "less than" on a number line means "to the left of." A "smaller" negative number is further away from zero than a "bigger" negative number. So the largest integer less than −2.3 is −3, and [−2.3] = −3. Notice that the result is **not** −2; this bracket operation is **not** truncation.

Be sure to follow the instructions exactly whenever you are given a special symbol or formula involving decimals. It is easy to jump to conclusions about how an operation works; for instance, finding the largest integer less than *x* is **not** the same as rounding *x* or truncating *x* in all cases. Also, do not confuse this particular set of brackets [*x*] with parentheses (*x*) or absolute value signs |*x*|.

Chemical Mixtures

Another type of GMAT percent problem bears mention: the chemical mixture problem:

> A 500 mL solution is 20% alcohol by volume. If 100 mL of water is added, what is the new concentration of alcohol, as a percent of volume?

Chemical mixture problems can be solved systematically by using a mixture chart:

Volume (mL)	Original	Change	New
Alcohol	100 mL	100 mL	1/6
Water	400 mL	500 mL	
Total Solution	500 mL	600 mL	

$$\frac{20}{100} = \frac{x}{500}$$

Note that Original + Change = New. Moreover, the rows contain the parts of the mixture and sum to a total. Only insert actual amounts; compute percents off on the side.

First, fill in the amounts that you know. Put 500 mL of solution in the Original column. You can also put +100 mL of water in the Change column. Since no alcohol was added or removed, put 0 mL of alcohol in the Change column. This tells you that our total Change is 100 mL as well. You do not need to input the units (mL):

Volume (mL)	Original	Change	New
Alcohol		0	
Water		+100	
Total Solution	500	+100	

Since the Original solution is 20% alcohol, you can compute the mL of alcohol in the Original solution by asking: How many mL of alcohol is 20% of 500 mL? Solve this using the decimal equivalent: $x = (0.20)(500 \text{ mL}) = 100 \text{ mL}$.

Now, fill in all the remaining numbers:

Volume (mL)	Original	Change	New
Alcohol	100	0	100
Water	400	+100	500
Total Solution	500	+100	600

Finally, you can find the new alcohol percentage: $\dfrac{\text{Alcohol}}{\text{Total}} = \dfrac{100}{600} = \dfrac{1}{6} \approx 0.167 = 16.7\%.$

Note that with this chart, you can handle proportions of many kinds. For instance, you might have been asked the concentration of water in the final solution. Simply take the quantities from the proper rows and columns and calculate a proportion.

Percents and Weighted Averages

A mixture chart can be used to solve weighted average problems that involve percents:

> Kris-P cereal is 10% sugar by weight, whereas healthier but less delicious Bran-O cereal is 2% sugar by weight. To make a delicious and healthy mixture that is 4% sugar, what should be the ratio of Kris-P cereal to Bran-O cereal, by weight?

First, set up a mixture chart. This time, instead of Original/Change/New, put the cereal brands and Total across the top. Also, put the parts of each cereal in the rows:

Pounds (lbs)	Kris-P	Bran-O	Total
Sugar			
Other stuff			
Total Cereal			

You are not given any actual weights in this problem, nor are you asked for any such weights. As a result, you can pick one Smart Number. Pick the total amount of Kris-P: 100 pounds (lbs). Now you can compute how much sugar is in that Kris-P: (0.10)(100) = 10 lbs. Do not bother computing the weight of the "other stuff"; it rarely matters.

Pounds (lbs)	Kris-P	Bran-O	Total
Sugar	10		
Other stuff			
Total Cereal	100		

Now set the total amount of Bran-O as x lb (you cannot pick another Smart Number). Since Bran-O is only 2% sugar, the mass of sugar in the Bran-O will be $(0.02)x$ lb. You can now add up the bottom row: the total amount of all cereals is $100 + x$ lb. Since the total mixture is 4% sugar, the weight of sugar in the mixture is $(0.04)(100 + x)$ lb:

Pounds (lbs)	Kris-P	Bran-O	Total
Sugar	10	$(0.02)x$	$(0.04)(100 + x)$
Other stuff			
Total Cereal	100	x	$100 + x$

Finally, you can write an equation summing the top row (the amounts of sugar):

$$10 + (0.02)x = (0.04)(100 + x) \qquad 6 = (0.02)x$$
$$10 + (0.02)x = 4 + (0.04)x \qquad 300 = x$$

The ratio of Kris-P to Bran-O is 100 : 300 or 1 : 3.

This result should make sense: to make a 4% mixture out of 10% and 2% cereals, you need much more of the 2%. In fact, 4% is the average of 10% and 2%, weighted 1 to 3.

7

Percent Change and Weighted Averages

Weighted averages can also show up in "percent change" problems:

> A company sells only pens and pencils. The revenue from pen sales in 2007 was up 5% from 2006, but the revenue from pencil sales declined 13% over the same period. If overall revenue was down 1% from 2006 to 2007, what was the ratio of pencil revenue to pen revenue in 2006?

First, set up a chart. You can use the Original/Change/New framework, but write 2006 and 2007 in the column headers. Write Pen and Pencil Revenue in the row headers:

Dollars ($)	2006	Change	2007
Pen Revenue			
Pencil Revenue			
Total Revenue			

As in the previous problem, you are not given any actual amounts (in this case, dollar revenue), nor are you asked for any such revenue in dollar terms. Rather, you are asked for a ratio of revenue. As a result, you can pick one Smart Number. Pick $100 for the 2006 Pen Revenue. Since that revenue went up 5%, the change is +$5, and the 2007 Pen Revenue is $105. Remember, all amounts are in some monetary unit (say, dollars):

Dollars ($)	2006	Change	2007
Pen Revenue	100	+5	105
Pencil Revenue			
Total Revenue			

Now set the 2006 Pencil Revenue equal to x. Remember, you cannot pick another Smart Number, since you do not know what the ratio of 2006 revenue will be. Since the Pencil Revenue went down 13%, the change in dollar terms is $-0.13x$, and the 2007 Pencil Revenue is $0.87x$ dollars.

You can also write the 2006 Total Revenue as the sum of that column. Since the Total Revenue went down 1%, the change (again, in dollar terms) is $-0.01(100 + x)$, and the 2007 Total Revenue is $0.99(100 + x)$:

Dollars ($)	2006	Change	2007
Pen Revenue	100	+5	105
Pencil Revenue	x	$-0.13x$	$0.87x$
Total Revenue	$100 + x$	$-0.01(100 + x)$	$0.99(100 + x)$

Finally, you can write an equation summing the 2007 column:

$$105 + 0.87x = 0.99(100 + x)$$
$$105 + 0.87x = 99 + 0.99x$$
$$6 = 0.12x$$
$$600 = 12x$$
$$50 = x$$

Since the 2006 Pen Revenue is $100, the ratio of Pencil Revenue to Pen Revenue in 2006 is $50:100$, or $1:2$.

Be sure to answer the question exactly as given! The problem could easily ask for the ratio of Pen Revenue to Pencil Revenue in 2007, or for the ratio of either part to the total.

Again, this result should make sense. A 5% increase in Pen Revenue and a 13% decline in Pencil Revenue only average to a 1% decline overall if there is proportionally more Pen Revenue to start with. If the 2006 revenue of pens and pencils were equal, then the average change would just be a straight average (arithmetic mean):

$$\frac{+5\% + (-13\%)}{2} = \frac{-8\%}{2} = -4\%$$

As it stands, however, the overall percent change is a *weighted* average of the two percent changes. The weights are the 2006 (original) revenues:

$$\frac{(+5\%)(100) + (-13\%)(50)}{100 + 50} = \frac{+5 - 6.5}{150} = \frac{-1.5}{150} = -1\%$$

You can use a similar formula to solve for the $50 and thus the revenue ratio. The algebraic steps are the same as they are with the chart:

$$\frac{(+5\%)(100) + (-13\%)(x)}{100 + x} = -1\%$$

In fact, to solve this equation for x, you can simply leave the percents as percents, rather than change them to decimals.

Last, do not forget that on any real GMAT problem, you can plug in answer choices. You will always be given the correct ratio in one of the answer choices. Simply pick an answer choice (say, a ratio of $1:3$) and invent revenues based on that ratio (say, $100:$300). Then work forward from there, finding the changes in revenue per product and overall revenue. Compare your results to the overall change given. Repeat as necessary. This method can be computationally intensive, but it will produce the correct answer eventually in many situations.

For more on Weighted Averages, see the *Word Problems* Strategy Guide.

Estimating Decimal Equivalents

When you are estimating the decimal equivalent of a fraction, you often have a few choices:

Estimate a decimal equivalent for $\dfrac{9}{52}$. (By long division, $\dfrac{9}{52} \approx 0.173077\ldots$)

Choice (1): Make the denominator the nearest factor of 100 or another power of 10:

$$\frac{9}{52} \approx \frac{9}{50} = \frac{18}{100} = 0.18 > \text{ real value} \qquad \text{High estimate: Lower the denominator.}$$

Choice (2): Change the numerator or denominator to make the fraction simplify easily:

$$\frac{9}{52} \approx \frac{9}{54} = \frac{1}{6} = 0.1\bar{6} < \text{ real value} \qquad \text{Low estimate: Raise the denominator.}$$

Try not to change both the numerator and denominator, especially in opposite directions. But in a pinch, you *can* adjust both numbers—especially if your estimation does not have to be that precise (e.g., in order to eliminate answers of a drastically different size):

$$\frac{9}{52} \approx\approx \frac{10}{50} = \frac{1}{5} = 0.2 \gg \text{ real value} \qquad \text{Raise the top } and \text{ lower the bottom.}$$

If you need a more precise estimate, you can average a couple of methods, or you can think about *small percent adjustments*:

Estimate $\dfrac{100{,}000}{96}$. (By the calculator, $\dfrac{100{,}000}{96} = 1{,}041.\bar{6}$)

First adjust the denominator to 100 and perform the division:

$$\frac{100{,}000}{96} \approx \frac{100{,}000}{100} = 1{,}000 < \text{real value} \quad \text{Raise the denominator.}$$

Now, you can make the following **approximation**, as long as you realize it is **never exact**, and that you can only use it for small adjustments. Use with caution!

You increased the denominator from 96 to 100. That is *approximately* a 4% increase:

$$\frac{\text{Change}}{\text{Original}} = \frac{4}{96} \approx \frac{4}{100}$$

This means that you can increase the result by 4%, to make your estimate more accurate:

$$1{,}000(1.04) = 1{,}040$$

Notice how close this estimate is to the real value (1,040 is 99.84% of $1{,}041.\bar{6}$).

Problem Set

1. What is the units digit of $\left(\dfrac{6^6}{6^5}\right)^6$?   6

2. What is the units digit of $(2)^5(3)^3(4)^2$?

3. What is the sum of all the possible three-digit numbers that can be constructed using the digits 3, 4, and 5 if each digit can be used only once in each number?

4. What is the length of the sequence of different digits in the decimal equivalent of $\dfrac{3}{7}$?

5. Which of the following fractions will terminate when expressed as a decimal? (Choose all that apply.)

    (A) $\dfrac{1}{256}$ (B) $\dfrac{27}{100}$ (C) $\dfrac{100}{27}$ (D) $\dfrac{231}{660}$ (E) $\dfrac{7}{105}$

6. Data Sufficiency: The number A is a two-digit positive integer; the number B is the two-digit positive integer formed by reversing the digits of A. If $Q = 10B - A$, what is the value of Q?

    (1) The tens digit of A is 7.
    (2) The tens digit of B is 6.

7.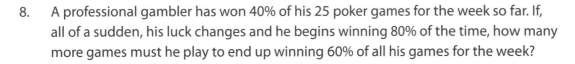

    In the multiplication above, each symbol represents a different unknown digit, and ● × ■ × ◆ = 36. What is the three-digit integer ●■◆?

    (A) 263   (B) 236   (C) 194   (D) 491   (E) 452

8. A professional gambler has won 40% of his 25 poker games for the week so far. If, all of a sudden, his luck changes and he begins winning 80% of the time, how many more games must he play to end up winning 60% of all his games for the week?

9. A feed store sells two varieties of birdseed: Brand A, which is 40% millet and 60% sunflower, and Brand B, which is 65% millet and 35% safflower. If a customer purchases a mix of the two types of birdseed that is 50% millet, what percent of the mix is Brand A?

10. A grocery store sells two varieties of jellybean jars, and each type of jellybean jar contains only red and yellow jellybeans. If Jar B contains 20% more red jellybeans than Jar A, but 10% fewer yellow jellybeans, and Jar A contains twice as many red jellybeans as yellow jellybeans, by what percent is the number of jellybeans in Jar B larger than the number of jellybeans in Jar A?

11. Last year, all registered voters in Kumannia voted either for the Revolutionary Party or for the Status Quo Party. This year, the number of Revolutionary voters increased 10%, while the number of Status Quo voters increased 5%. No other votes were cast. If the number of total voters increased 8%, what fraction of voters voted Revolutionary this year?

12. A large tub is filled with 920 units of alcohol and 1,800 units of water. 40% of the water evaporates. What percent of the remaining liquid is water?

13. Order from least to greatest:

$$\frac{\frac{3}{5}}{\frac{8}{10}} \qquad \frac{0.00751}{0.01} \qquad \frac{200}{3}\times10^{-2}$$

14. Estimate the following fractions in terms of decimals, and note whether your estimate is greater than or less than the real value:

$$\frac{12}{37} \qquad \frac{14}{90} \qquad \frac{13}{51} \qquad \frac{168}{839}$$

Solutions

1. **6:** First, use the rules for combining exponents to simplify the expression. Subtract the exponents to get $\dfrac{6^6}{6^5}$. Then, raise this to the sixth power: $6^6 = 6^2 \times 6^2 \times 6^2 = 36 \times 36 \times 36$. Ignore any digits other than the last one: $6 \times 6 \times 6 = 36 \times 6$. Again, ignore any digits other than the last one: $6 \times 6 = 36$. The last digit is 6.

2. **4:** Use the Last Digit Shortcut, ignoring all digits but the last in any intermediate products:

Step 1: $2^5 = 32$ Drop the tens digit and keep only the last digit: 2.
Step 2: $3^3 = 27$ Drop the tens digit and keep only the last digit: 7.
Step 3: $4^2 = 16$ Drop the tens digit and keep only the last digit: 6.
Step 4: $2 \times 7 \times 6 = 84$ Drop the tens digit and keep only the last digit: 4.

3. **2664:** There are 6 ways in which to arrange these digits: 345, 354, 435, 453, 534, and 543. Notice that each digit appears twice in the hundreds column, twice in the tens column, and twice in the ones column. Therefore, you can use your knowledge of place value to find the sum quickly. Because each digit appears twice in the hundreds column, you have $3 + 3 + 4 + 4 + 5 + 5 = 24$ in the hundreds column. If you multiply 24 by 100, you get the value of all of the numbers in that column. Repeat this reasoning for the tens column and the ones column:

$$100(24) + 10(24) + (24) = 2400 + 240 + 24 = 2664.$$

4. **6:** Generally, the easiest way to find the pattern of digits in a non-terminating decimal is to simply do the long division and wait for the pattern to repeat (see long division at right). This results in a repeating pattern of $0.\overline{428571}$.

```
       0.4285714
   7 ) 3.0000000
       0
       ---
       3.0
       2.8
       ----
        20
       -14
       ----
        60
       -56
       ----
         40
        -35
        ----
         50
        -49
        ----
          10
          -7
         ----
          30
         -28
         ----
           2
```

5. **(A), (B), and (D):** Recall that in order for the decimal version of a fraction to terminate, the fraction's denominator in fully reduced form must have a prime factorization that consists of only 2's and/or 5's. The denominator in (A) is composed of only 2's ($256 = 2^8$). The denominator in (B) is composed of only 2's and 5's ($100 = 2^2 \times 5^2$). In fully reduced form, the fraction in (D) is equal to $\dfrac{7}{20}$, and 20 is composed of only 2's and 5's ($20 = 2^2 \times 5$). By contrast, the denominator in (C) has prime factors other than 2's and 5's ($27 = 3^3$), and in fully reduced form, the fraction in (E) is equal to $\dfrac{1}{15}$, and 15 has a prime factor other than 2's and 5's ($15 = 3 \times 5$).

6. **(B) Statement (2) ALONE is sufficient, but statement (1) alone is NOT sufficient:** Write A as XY, where X and Y are digits (X is the tens digit of A and Y is the units digit of A). Then B can be written as YX, with reversed digits. Writing these numbers in algebraic rather than digital form, you have $A = 10X + Y$ and $B = 10Y + X$. Therefore, $Q = 10B - A = 10(10Y + X) - (10X + Y) = 100Y + 10X - 10X - Y = 99Y$. The

value of Q only depends on the value of Y, which is the tens digit of B. The value of X is irrelevant to Q. Therefore, statement (2) alone is SUFFICIENT.

You can also make up and test numbers to get the same result, but algebra is faster and more transparent. For instance, if you take $Y = 7$, then $Q = 693$, which contains no 7's digits. Thus, it may be hard to see how Q depends on Y.

7. **(B):** The three symbols ●, ■, and ◆ multiply to 36 and each must represent a different digit. Break 36 into its primes: $2 \times 2 \times 3 \times 3$. What three different digits can you create using two 2s and two 3s? 2, 3, and 6. So these three symbols (●, ■, and ◆) must equal 2, 3, and 6, but which is which? (Note: At this point, only (A) or (B) can be the answer.) Notice in the multiplication problem given that the unit's digit indicates that ◆ × ◆ = ◆. Which of the three numbers will give this result? Only the number 6 ($6 \times 6 = 36$; the unit's digit is the same). So the ◆ must equal 6 and the unit's digit of ●■◆ must be 6. Only answer choice (B) fits this requirement.

8. **25 more games:** This is a weighted averages problem. You can set up a table to calculate the number of games he must play to obtain a weighted average win rate of 60%:

Poker Games	First 25 Games	Remaining Games	Total
Wins	(0.4)25 = 10	(0.8)x	(0.6)(25 + x)
Losses			
Total	25	x	25 + x

Thus, $10 + 0.8x = (0.6)(25 + x)$, $10 + 0.8x = 15 + 0.6x$, $0.2x = 5$, $x = 25$.

9. **60%:** This is a weighted averages problem. You can set up a table to calculate the answer, and assume that you purchased 100 lbs of Brand A:

Pounds (lbs)	Brand A	Brand B	Total
Millet	40	0.65x	(0.5)(100 + x)
Other stuff	60	0.35x	(0.5)(100 + x)
Total birdseed	100	x	100 + x

Thus, $40 + 0.65x = (0.5)(100 + x)$, $40 + 0.65x = 50 + 0.5x$, $0.15x = 10$, $x = \dfrac{1,000}{15}$.

Therefore, Brand A is $\dfrac{100}{100 + \dfrac{1,000}{15}} = \dfrac{100}{\dfrac{1,500}{15} + \dfrac{1,000}{15}} = \dfrac{1,500}{2,500} = 60\%$ of the total.

10. **10%:** This is a weighted average "percent change" problem. You can set up a table to calculate the answer, and assume that Jar A contains 200 red jellybeans and 100 yellow jellybeans:

Jellybeans	Jar A	Difference	Jar B
Red	200	+40	200(1.2) = 240
Yellow	100	−10	100(0.9) = 90
Total Jellybeans	300	+30	240 + 90 = 330

Thus, Jar B has $\dfrac{30}{300}$, or 10%, more jellybeans than Jar A.

11. $\dfrac{11}{18}$: This is a weighted average "percent change" problem. You can set up a table to calculate the answer, and assume that last year there were 100 Revolutionary voters:

Voters	Last Year	This Year	Total
Revolutionary	100	+10	100(1.1) = 110
Status Quo	x	+0.05x	x(1.05) = 1.05x
Total Voters	100 + x	+0.08(100 + x)	110 + 1.05x

Thus, $100 + x + 0.08(100 + x) = 110 + 1.05x$, $108 + 1.08x = 110 + 1.05x$.

$0.03x = 2$ $\qquad x = \dfrac{2}{0.03} = \dfrac{200}{3}$

Thus, for every 100 Revolutionary voters last year, there were approximately 67 Status Quo voters. The question, however, asks you to compute the percentage of voters who voted Revolutionary *this* year. Thus, the number of Revolutionary voters this year is $(100)(1.1) = 110$, and the number of Status Quo voters this year is $\dfrac{200}{3}(1.05) = \dfrac{210}{3} = 70$. Therefore, $\dfrac{110}{110+70} = \dfrac{110}{180} = \dfrac{11}{18}$ of voters, or approximately 61.1%, voted Revolutionary this year.

12. **54%:** For this liquid mixture problem, set up a table with two columns: one for the original mixture and one for the mixture after the water evaporates from the tub:

	Original	After Evaporation
Alcohol	920	920
Water	1,800	0.60(1,800) = 1,080
Total	2,720	2,000

The remaining liquid in the tub is $\dfrac{1,080}{2,000}$, or 54%, water.

You could also solve for the new amount of water using the formula:

$$\text{Original} \times \left(1 - \dfrac{\text{Percent Decrease}}{100}\right) = \text{New}$$

$$1{,}800\left(1-\frac{40}{100}\right)=(1{,}800)(0.6)=1{,}080 \text{ units of water. Water is } \frac{1{,}080}{920+1{,}080}=\frac{1{,}080}{2{,}000}=54\% \text{ of the}$$

total.

13. $\dfrac{200}{3}\times 10^{-2} < \dfrac{3}{5}\div\dfrac{8}{10} < \dfrac{0.00751}{0.01}$

First, simplify all terms and express them in decimal form:

$$\frac{3}{5}\div\frac{8}{10}=\frac{3}{5}\times\frac{10}{8}=\frac{3}{4}=0.75$$

$$\frac{0.00751}{0.01}=\frac{0.751}{1}=0.751$$

$$\frac{200}{3}\times 10^{-2}=\frac{200}{3}\times\frac{1}{10^{2}}=\frac{200}{3}\times\frac{1}{100}=\frac{2}{3}=0.\overline{6}$$

$$0.\overline{6}<0.75<0.751$$

14. To estimate a fraction, you can either change the denominator to a nearby factor of 10, or change either the denominator or numerator to make the fraction easy to reduce. There is no "correct" way to do this, but the closer to the real value, the better:

$\dfrac{12}{37}$: Either change the denominator to $\dfrac{12}{36}=\dfrac{1}{3}=0.\overline{3}$, a slight overestimate (because you reduced the denominator), or to $\dfrac{12}{40}=\dfrac{3}{10}=0.3$, a slight underestimate (because you increased the denominator).

$\dfrac{14}{90}$: Either change the denominator to $\dfrac{14}{100}=0.14$, an underestimate (because you increased the denominator), or to $\dfrac{15}{90}=\dfrac{1}{6}=0.1\overline{6}$, an overestimate (because you increased the numerator).

$\dfrac{13}{51}$: Either change the denominator to $\dfrac{13}{52}=\dfrac{1}{4}=0.25$, an underestimate (because you increased the denominator), or to $\dfrac{13}{50}=0.26$, an overestimate (because you reduced the denominator).

$\dfrac{168}{839}$: Best is to change the denominator to $\dfrac{168}{840}=\dfrac{21}{105}=\dfrac{1}{5}=0.2$, a very slight underestimate (because you increased the denominator). Similarly, you might switch the fraction to $\dfrac{170}{850}=\dfrac{17}{85}=\dfrac{1}{5}=0.2$, although because you increased both the numerator and denominator slightly, it is hard to tell whether this would be an underestimate or overestimate. If you missed those relationships, you could change the fraction to $\dfrac{168}{800}=0.21$, a slight overestimate (because you reduced the denominator).

Appendix A

of

Fractions, Decimals, & Percents

Official Guide Problem Sets

In This Chapter...

Official Guide Problem Sets

Problem Solving Set

Data Sufficiency Set

Official Guide Problem Sets

Now that you have completed *Fractions, Decimals, & Percents*, it is time to test your skills on problems that have actually appeared on real GMAT exams over the past several years.

The problem sets that follow are composed of questions from two books published by the Graduate Management Admission Council® (the organization that develops the official GMAT exam):

> *The Official Guide for GMAT Review, 13th Edition*
> *The Official Guide for GMAT Quantitative Review, 2nd Edition*

These books contain quantitative questions that have appeared on past official GMAT exams. (The questions contained therein are the property of The Graduate Management Admission Council, which is not affiliated in any way with Manhattan GMAT.)

Although the questions in *The Official Guides* have been "retired" (they will not appear on future official GMAT exams), they are great practice questions.

In order to help you practice effectively, we have categorized every problem in *The Official Guides* by topic and subtopic. On the following pages, you will find two categorized lists:

1. **Problem Solving:** Lists Problem Solving Fractions, Decimals, & Percents questions contained in *The Official Guides* and categorizes them by subtopic.

2. **Data Sufficiency:** Lists Data Sufficiency Fractions, Decimals, & Percents questions contained in *The Official Guides* and categorizes them by subtopic.

Books 1 through 8 of Manhattan GMAT's Strategy Guide series each contain a unique *Official Guide* list that pertains to the specific topic of that particular book. If you complete all the practice problems contained on the *Official Guide* lists in each of these 8 Manhattan GMAT Strategy Guide books, you will have completed every single question published in *The Official Guides*.

Problem Solving Set

This set is from *The Official Guide for GMAT Review, 13th Edition* (pages 20–23 & 152–185), and *The Official Guide for GMAT Quantitative Review, 2nd Edition* (pages 62–86).

Solve each of the following problems in a notebook, making sure to demonstrate how you arrived at each answer by showing all of your work and computations. If you get stuck on a problem, look back at the Fractions, Decimals, & Percents strategies and content contained in this guide to assist you.

Note: Problem numbers preceded by "D" refer to questions in the Diagnostic Test chapter of *The Official Guide for GMAT Review, 13th Edition* (pages 20–23).

Digits & Decimals:

13th Edition: 17, 20, 65, 85, 111, 122, 142, 146, 156, 163, 170, 212, 218, 227, D1, D11
Quantitative Review: 4, 6, 65, 93, 174

Fractions:

13th Edition: 15, 27, 41, 46, 48, 80, 97, 108, 151, 194, 195, 209, 214, 226, D8
Quantitative Review: 8, 14, 39, 42, 46, 48, 50, 53, 59, 60, 61, 69, 88, 118, 128, 134, 165, 167, 176

Percents:

13th Edition: 6, 11, 19, 21, 31, 57, 58, 59, 71, 84, 94, 96, 114, 115, 123, 135, 141, 144, 152, 171, 177, 181, 182, 185, 198, 201, 224, D12, D21
Quantitative Review: 9, 10, 12, 26, 34, 35, 38, 43, 49, 66, 73, 89, 95, 100, 101, 114, 120, 138, 143, 154, 155, 159

Ratios:

13th Edition: 22, 56, 63, 66, 82, 98, 105, 113, 125, 179, 188, 200
Quantitative Review: 82

FDPs:

13th Edition: 8
Quantitative Review: 27, 29, 45, 58

Data Sufficiency Set

This set is from *The Official Guide for GMAT Review, 13th Edition* (pages 24–26 & 274–291), and *The Official Guide for GMAT Quantitative Review, 2nd Edition* (pages 152–163).

Solve each of the following problems in a notebook, making sure to demonstrate how you arrived at each answer by showing all of your work and computations. If you get stuck on a problem, look back at the Fractions, Decimals, & Percents strategies and content contained in this guide to assist you.

Practice **rephrasing** both the questions and the statements. The majority of data sufficiency problems can be rephrased; however, if you have difficulty rephrasing a problem, try testing numbers to solve it. It is especially important that you familiarize yourself with the directions for data sufficiency problems, and that you memorize the 5 fixed answer choices that accompany all data sufficiency problems.

Note: Problem numbers preceded by "D" refer to questions in the Diagnostic Test chapter of *The Official Guide for GMAT Review, 13th Edition* (pages 24–26).

Digits & Decimals:

13th Edition: 31, 63, 75, 80, 104, 133, 157, 170, D25
Quantitative Review: 21, 30, 44, 49, 96, 102, 104

Fractions:

13th Edition: 10, 29, 92, 116, 131
Quantitative Review: 2, 48, 119

Percents:

13th Edition: 2, 8, 25, 40, 55, 61, 62, 76, 91, 94, 127, 150, D40
Quantitative Review: 5, 36, 50, 53, 75, 93

Ratios:

13th Edition: 23, 26, 47, 81, 114, 161, 168
Quantitative Review: 67, 77

FDPs:

13th Edition: 46, 51, 88, 148, 151

mbaMission